EnglishSmart – Contents

MW01610458

1 **The Sentence and Its Parts**
— Subjects & Predicates • Verbs & Simple Subjects • Direct & Indirect Objects • Definite & Indefinite Articles
2

2 **Nouns and Pronouns**
— Types of Nouns • Types of Pronouns
6

3 **Adjectives and Adverbs**
— Predicate Adjectives • Possessive Adjectives • Adjective and Adverb Phrases
10

4 **Clauses**
— Dependent & Independent Clauses • Subordinate Conjunctions • Adjective & Adverb Clauses • Noun Clauses
14

5 **Verb Tenses**
— Tenses: Progressive, Perfect, Perfect Progressive • Transitive & Intransitive Verbs • Problem Verbs
18

6 **Verbals and Verbal Phrases**
— Present & Past Participles • Participle Phrases . Gerunds • Gerund Phrases • Infinitives • Infinitive Phrases
22

7 **Direct and Indirect (Reported) Speech**
— Direct Speech • Change of Time Reference • Indirect Questions
26

Progress Test 1
30

8 **Building Sentences**
— Sentence Combining • Problem Sentences • Comma Splice
36

9 **The Comma, the Colon, and the Semicolon**
— Commas for Non-Restrictive Adjective Clauses & Nouns in Apposition • The Colon • The Semicolon
40

10 **Dashes, Hyphens, Brackets, and Parentheses**
— The Dash • The Hyphen • Brackets • Parentheses • Other Structural Devices
44

11 **Varying Sentence Construction**
— Using Phrases to Begin a Sentence • Inverting Word Order • Building Detailed Sentences
48

12 **Paragraph Construction**
— The Paragraph • Expanding the Topic Sentence • Making Headlines
52

13 **Tips for Effective Writing**
— Frequently Confused Words • Padded Language • Faulty Sentences • Faulty Parallels • Mixed Construction
56

14 **The Descriptive Paragraph**
— Descriptive Language • Spatial Order • From General to Specific
60

15 **The Narrative and Explanatory Composition**
— The Narrative Composition • The Explanatory Composition
64

Progress Test 2
68

Answers
75

1 The Sentence and Its Parts

A sentence is a group of words that expresses a complete thought or idea. It may make a statement of fact, give a command, or ask a question.

A basic sentence is made up of two parts: **a subject** and **a predicate**.

The **subject** contains the subject of the sentence, usually a noun, and its modifiers.

The **predicate** is made up of a verb, the action being performed, and its modifiers.

Exercise A

Underline the complete subject in each sentence below, and place parentheses ( ) around the predicate.

> One sentence below is a compound sentence and has two subjects and two predicates. Do you recognize which sentence it is?

1. The fluffy, white clouds drifted lazily overhead.
2. The boy's bicycle was locked in the backyard.
3. Boys and girls alike enjoyed watching the movie.
4. Cows, sheep, and chickens shared the same barn on the farm.
5. To win is exciting but to play fair is most important.
6. The morning of our first day on holiday was bleak.
7. Playing baseball, basketball, and football are his favourite activities.

Exercise B

Sentences must express a complete thought. Write "Complete" or "Incomplete" after each group of words below.

1. His dog likes to swim in the lake.   Complete
2. Whenever we go to a restaurant.   INcomplete
3. Her eyes turned red.   complete
4. It is bitterly cold in Quebec during winter.   complete
5. If they invite us.   INcomplete
6. A walk in the park.   INcomplete
7. Walking through the forest.   INcomplete

Exercise C

Add your own words to turn the incomplete sentences in Exercise B into complete ones.

Whenever we go to the resterant we eat alot.

If they invite us it will be fun.

a walk in the park would be nice.

Walking through the forest

Verbs and Simple Subjects

A verb represents the action of the subject in a sentence. The simple subject (bare subject) is a noun or pronoun that performs the action of the verb.

Example: The boy rode his bicycle.
"Boy" is the simple subject and "rode" is the verb.

Exercise D

Underline the simple subject and place parentheses ( ) around the verb in each sentence below.

The order of some of the sentences may be inverted; that is, the subject may not appear first.

1. The frightened boy (ran) from the barking dog.
2. Swiftly, the river current (swept) away the boat.
3. In order to see better, they (changed) seats.
4. The car was (washed) by the students raising money for a school trip.
5. Under the shade of the old oak tree, they (had) their picnic.
6. During the night, the wind (blew) the roof off the shed.
7. Leo never (saw) his cat again.
8. Never have I (seen) such a huge snake before.
9. (Slowly) but surely, the little boy walked into the room.
10. After the party, the guests helped (tidy) up everything.

Direct and Indirect Objects in a Sentence

A direct object is the direct receiver of the action of the verb. A verb that directs action to a direct object is called a transitive verb.

Example: He kicked the **ball** into the net.
The "ball" is the receiver of the action of the verb "kicked". The verb "kicked" is a transitive verb because it directs action to the object "ball".

An indirect object tells to whom or to what, or for whom or for what the action of the verb is directed. The indirect object does not receive the action of the verb directly.

Example: His father made **them** hamburgers for lunch.
The word "hamburgers" is the direct object because it represents what receives the direct action of the verb. The word "them" is the indirect object because it tells to whom the action is indirectly forwarded.

Exercise E

Underline the direct objects and place parentheses ( ) around the indirect objects in the sentences below.

1. The player passed him the (puck) skilfully.

2. The teacher asked us many interesting (questions.)

3. The water (soaked) us thoroughly.

4. The music teacher sang us a (song.)

5. The store gave new customers a free (gift.)

6. John asked Paul a (question.)

Definite and Indefinite Articles

Articles, also known as noun determiners, are adjectives that always precede the noun they modify. Essentially, they identify which noun is referred to or they tell that a noun is singular. "A", "an", and "the" are articles.

Example (1): He gave **the** teacher **an** apple.
The teacher is a specific person (the), whereas the apple is a non-specific noun because it is described as "an" apple, and not "the" apple.

Example (2): He gave **a** teacher **the** apple.
The apple is specific and the teacher is non-specific.

If two or more nouns refer to one person, do not repeat the article.
For example: He was well-known as a poet and singer.

Exercise F

Insert the proper article in the following sentences from the choices in parentheses.

1. He waited ___an___ (a, an) hour for the bus.
2. She placed ___the___ (the, a) red sweater that she bought today on a hanger.
3. Give him ___an___ (a, an) egg for breakfast.
4. The story was ___a___ (a, an) hoax.
5. He placed his hat on ___an___ (a, an) upper shelf.
6. This was ___a___ (a, an) unique event.
7. She loves ___a___ (a, an) good book with ___an___ (a, an) interesting story.
8. In hiring Mr. Smith, the school got ___an___ (a, an) experienced teacher and coach.

Exercise G

Assemble the following words and phrases to make understandable sentences.

> Don't forget to place a capital letter at the beginning and a period at the end.

1. a basketball game / after school / yesterday / watched / we / in the gym

   ___Yester day after school we a basketball game in the gym___

2. our school team / with the best record / the team / against / played

   ___Our school team played against the team with the best record___

3. did not / fell behind / our team / give up / they / although

   ___Our did not give up although they fell behind___

4. they / three points / trailed / in the last minute / by only / of the last quarter

   ___they trailed by only three points in the last minute of last quarter___

5. the long shot / and / lost the game / Ken / unfortunately / missed / our team

   ___The long shot unfortunately missed our team lost the game___

6. our team / in spite of / well / played / the / loss / very

   ___In spite of the loss our team played very well.___

2 Nouns and Pronouns

There are four types of nouns: common, proper, concrete, and abstract.

Common Nouns: nouns that name non-specific persons, places, things, or ideas
Examples: house, yard, bicycle, bottle, thoughts, feelings
Proper Nouns: nouns that name specific persons, places, things, or ideas
Examples: Will Smith, Wayne Gretzky, Vancouver, Newfoundland, Kleenex
Concrete Nouns: nouns that can be recognized by the senses (see, hear, feel, taste)
Examples: music, heat, sunset, cream, garlic
Abstract Nouns: nouns that name ideas, concepts, qualities, beliefs, ideals
Examples: love, hatred, kindness, imagination, creativity, happiness

Exercise A

Nouns are used as the subject and the object in a sentence.

Fill in the blanks with appropriate nouns.

1. The _____ gathered in the _____ for a game of soccer.

2. They ordered _____ , hot dogs, ice cream, and cake for _____ .

3. Mohammad Ali was a famous _____ and world _____ .

4. The _____ was named Willow Avenue because of the trees that grew there.

5. To achieve _____ is a goal that many people share.

Compound Nouns

Nouns that are made up of more than one word are called compound nouns. These words may be formed by joining two nouns together by a hyphen or by forming a single word. They may also be formed by simply placing two nouns together.

Exercise B

Match the nouns below to form compound nouns.

1.	fire	•	•	pool	2.	father	•	•	room
3.	man	•	•	quarters	4.	dining	•	•	plant
5.	swimming	•	•	place	6.	egg	•	•	dryer
7.	head	•	•	hole	8.	hair	•	•	-in-law

Rules for Plural Form of Nouns

1. Add **s** to most singular nouns.
2. Certain nouns ending in **f**, **fe**, and **ff** form plurals by simply adding **s** to the singular form; for other nouns ending in **f** or **fe**, change the **f** to **v** and add **es**.
3. Nouns that end in **ch, s, sh, z,** and **x** form plurals by adding **es** to the singular.
4. For nouns that end in **y** – when the **y** is preceded by a consonant, change the **y** to **i** and add **es**; for nouns that end in y – when the **y** is preceded by a vowel, add **s** to the singular (except for nouns that end in **quy**).
5. For most nouns ending in **o** preceded by a vowel, simply add **s** to the singular; for most nouns ending in **o** preceded by a consonant, add **es**.

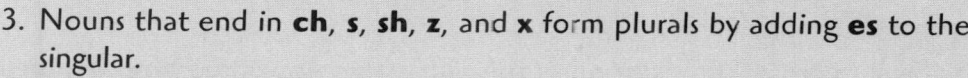

There are often exceptions to the rules.

Exercise C

Circle the correct plural form for the nouns below.

1. chief – chieves   chiefs
2. tax – taxs   taxes
3. proof – proofs   proofes   proves
4. army – armies   armys
5. shelf – shelfs   shelves
6. sky – skys   skies   skyes
7. church – churchs   churches
8. radio – radioes   radios
9. keys – keyes   keys
10. hero – heroes   heros
11. patio – patioes   patios
12. six – sixs   sixes

CHALLENGE

1. What do these nouns have in common:
   sheep   moose   deer   salmon   grass?

   Answer: _____

2. Some nouns have two plural forms for different meanings. Give a definition for each of these plural nouns:

   cloths _____

   clothes _____

3. Do these plural nouns take a singular or plural verb?

   The news _____ (is/are) interesting.
   Measles _____ (is/are) an illness.

Pronouns fall into three categories: **Subjective**, **Objective**, and **Possessive**.

Subjective Pronouns are used as:

1. the subject of a sentence – **You** and **I** will go shopping for groceries.

2. a predicate complement following the verb to be (is, are, was, were) – I knew it was **you** who called. It was **he** who arrived too late.

Objective Pronouns are used as:

1. the object (receiver of the action) of the verb – They appointed **him** class president.

2. the indirect object of the verb – He asked **her** a question.

3. the object of a preposition – The gift came from **her**. (preposition – from)

Possessive Pronouns are used to:

1. show possession – This was **his** book. **My** friend called today.

2. complete the predicate – The decision was **his**. (used with the verb "be")

Exercise D

Fill in the missing pronouns.

After school, Jason and I rushed to the park for a game of baseball with

1. _____ friends. When 2. _____ arrived, 3. _____ were

already into the second inning. Jason's brother, Jeremy, was at the plate.

With bases loaded, 4. _____ had two strikes. 5. _____ instinct

told 6. _____ that 7. _____ could expect a fastball. Then a fastball

came right into the middle of the plate. 8. _____ swung hard at

9. _____ . The ball shot over the fence and disappeared into the woods.

10. _____ was a grand slam! 11. _____ teammates were so excited

that 12. _____ cheered wildly for 13. _____ . Jeremy felt really proud

as 14. _____ rounded the bases slowly because 15. _____ was the first

time 16. _____ had hit a grand slam.

Relative Pronouns

A relative pronoun connects a dependent (subordinate) clause to the main clause.

Example (1): The class **that** she was placed in was in another building.
Example (2): The book **which** you borrowed from school is due back on Friday.
Example (3): The new teacher **who** will be teaching grade 6 will coach baseball.

"That" refers to animals, persons, and things; "who" refers to persons only. The pronoun "who" takes on other forms: whose, whom, whoever, whomever.

In the subjective case use "who", "whoever"; in the objective case use "whom", "whomever".

Example (1): They talked to all the students **who** were going on the school trip.
  In this sentence, the relative pronoun is in the **subjective** case.
Example (2): They asked to **whom** you were speaking.
  In this sentence, the relative pronoun "whom" is in the **objective** case because it is the object of the preposition "to".

Exercise E

In each sentence below, select the correct pronoun to suit the sentence.

1. The puppy _____ (that, whom) we saw this morning belongs to Zoe.

2. I don't know to _____ (who, whom) you're referring.

3. He thanked the student _____ (who, that) volunteered to help.

4. The teacher named all the students _____ (which, that) were on the team.

5. He gave the news to _____ (whoever, whomever) was interested.

6. The animals _____ (that, who) were in the zoo were well taken care of.

7. The class laughed at the students _____ (who, whom) acted in the skit.

8. At _____ (which, whose) stop will the special bus pick up passengers?

> Interrogative pronouns are used to ask questions.

9. To _____ (who, whom) are you speaking?

10. _____ (What, Who) day did you arrive?

11. _____ (Whom, Who) lives next door to you?

12. For _____ (who, whom) did you bake the cake?

3 Adjectives and Adverbs

An **Adjective** may be placed close to the noun it describes, or it may appear in the predicate as a predicate adjective.

Example (1): He had a **delicious** dinner.
"Delicious" is an adjective describing the noun "dinner" and is placed next to the noun.

Example (2): The girl was **excited** about playing in the game.
"Excited" describes the noun "girl", but since it is located in the predicate part of the sentence, it is a predicate adjective.

Exercise A

Fill in each blank with an adjective of your choice.

1. The _____ children played on the swings.

2. The tired and _____ participants carried their _____ bags.

3. The red car circled the driveway of the _____ mansion.

4. She was delighted to be helping the _____ people.

5. The _____ , hungry lion was chasing the _____ hare .

6. I have never seen such a _____ movie before.

7. The _____ weather would last a few more days.

Predicate Adjectives

There are two kinds of predicate adjectives:
1. Descriptive words following verbs "to be" (is, are, was, were).
   Example: He is **tall**. ("Tall" is a predicate adjective.)
2. Descriptive words following verbs that refer to the senses.
   Example: She appears **happy** to be here. ("Happy" is an adjective although it is next to the verb; it follows a verb of one of the senses.)

Exercise B

Underline the predicate adjective in each sentence below.

1. The northerly wind feels chilly.

2. The green apple tasted sour.

3. The twin sisters were content to stay home.

4. The tall girl looks younger than my sister.

5. I am positive that she has eaten my candy.

6. Jasmine has been ill for quite some time.

7. The fruit cake that the girls made smells good.

8. The teacher was not happy about Dan's mischief.

Possessive Adjectives describe nouns and gerunds (verbals used as nouns). The following words are possessive adjectives: my, our, your, their, his, her, its.

 **Exercise C**

Add an appropriate possessive adjective to each sentence below.

1. I am going to take _____ dog for a walk this evening.

2. They carried _____ books in a knapsack.

3. Naomi called _____ mother but she was not at home.

4. We have forgotten where _____ tickets are kept.

5. He is arrogant but _____ twin brother is nice and friendly.

6. The naughty kitten played with _____ tail.

An adverb describes a verb (the action) in a sentence. Adverbs often end in "ly".

But two in the exercise below don't end in "ly".

 **Exercise D**

Underline all the adverbs in each of the sentences below. The numbers in parentheses indicates the number of adverbs in each sentence.

1. They ran fast and won the race. (1)

2. The swimmer moved gracefully in the pool. (1)

3. Swiftly but carefully, he walked across the road. (2)

4. The light shone brightly and the insects flew quickly towards it. (2)

5. They will eventually reach their destination. (1)

6. Ian did not work hard and he scored poorly on the exam. (2)

CHALLENGE

What is unusual about the underlined words in these sentences?

1. The hotel was <u>far</u> from the city and a <u>far</u> cry from what they expected.
2. He liked to drive the <u>fast</u> car <u>fast</u>.
3. The <u>first</u> student spoke <u>first</u> in front of the class.

Answer: _____

Adjective and Adverb Phrases

An adverb phrase acts as an adverb in a sentence; an adjective phrase acts as an adjective in a sentence. They modify verbs and nouns respectively.

Example (1): He placed the boots **under the stairway**.
"Under the stairway" is an adverb phrase introduced by the preposition "under". It describes **where** the boots were placed.

Example (2): The students **of the public school** went **on a class trip**.
"Of the public school" is an adjective phrase introduced by the preposition "of". It describes **what kind** of students they were.

"On a class trip" is an adverb phrase introduced by the preposition "on". It describes **where** they went.

Exercise E

Unscramble the following groups of words to make adjective and adverb phrases. Write a sentence using the phrase to describe either a verb or noun.

Where there are two groups of words, try to use both phrases in the same sentence.

1. sky, in, the, up

   _____

2. game, the, during   grade, of, sixth, the

   _____

3. morning, the, in, early   park, the, in, local

   _____

Exercise F

Create adverb and adjective phrases for the sentences below. Place your phrases in the spaces provided following the prepositions in italics.

1. The player *with* _____ walked over *to* _____ .

2. *At* _____ , we ate lunch, and then we went swimming *in* _____ .

3. *After* _____ , the weather was nice and sunny.

4. The students *from* _____ arrived *at* _____ .

5. He threw the ball *over* _____ and *across* _____ .

Exercise G

Fill in the superlative and comparative form chart below. There is a mix of adjective and adverb forms.

> The words with an asterisk (*) are irregular in comparative and superlative form.

> To form the comparative and superlative forms of some adverbs, and of adjectives with two syllables or more, use auxiliary (helping) words such as: more, most, less, least.

Regular	Comparative	Superlative
1. bad*	_____	_____
2. well*	_____	_____
3. lazily	_____	_____
4. useful	_____	_____
5. friendly	_____	_____
6. far*	_____	_____
7. good*	_____	_____
8. little*	_____	_____
9. much*	_____	_____

4 Clauses

Dependent and Independent Clauses

Clauses can be independent, which means they can stand alone. A sentence is an independent clause.

Clauses can also be dependent, which means they cannot stand on their own and need to be supported by an independent clause.

Exercise A

Identify the clauses below as dependent or independent. Place DEP (dependent) or IND (independent) in the spaces provided.

> Dependent clauses are also called subordinate clauses.

1. Pauline fell off her bicycle. _____
2. She was wearing a helmet. _____
3. Although she was not seriously injured. _____
4. She lay there for a while to recover. _____
5. If she had not put on a helmet. _____
6. Whenever we go cycling. _____

Subordinate Conjunctions

Independent clauses and dependent clauses are joined by subordinate conjunctions. Here is a list of some common subordinate conjunctions: as, since, now that, though, even though, if, even if, where, whereas, wherever, so that, in order that, after, whenever, till, until, while...

Exercise B

Finish each of the incomplete sentences by creating a clause to follow the italicized subordinating conjunction.

1. *Whenever* I eat too much, _____ .
2. He was happy to join the team *even though* _____ .
3. The school is much larger *since* _____ .
4. We waited at the bus stop *until* _____ .
5. They won the game *although* _____ .
6. She practised swimming every day *in order that* _____ .

Exercise C

Join each of the clauses in Column A to a clause in Column B to form a complex sentence. Write the newly formed sentences in the spaces provided and add commas where necessary.

Column A

1. The teacher was not happy
2. As we approached the beach
3. Even if we got up early
4. Because of the snowfall
5. After we finished eating dinner
6. Wherever we move to
7. She put on her raincoat
8. The best team will win the game
9. The school built a new gymnasium
10. It wasn't the best day for a picnic

Column B

- even though it wasn't raining yet.
- because the original one was too small.
- we will buy a new house.
- because our homework was sloppy.
- we would have been too late.
- provided that they play their best.
- we could feel the ocean breeze.
- the cars were sliding off the road.
- since we forgot the sandwiches.
- we had a delicious dessert.

1. _____

2. _____

3. _____

4. _____

5. _____

6. _____

7. _____

8. _____

9. _____

10. _____

Adjective and Adverb Clauses

An adjective clause acts as an adjective in a sentence – modifying a noun or pronoun.

Example: His decision, **which came as a great surprise**, shocked everyone.
The boldfaced adjective clause modifies the noun "decision".

Most adjective clauses begin with a relative pronoun such as "who", "which", "that", "whose", or "whom". However, some begin with "why", "where", or "when".

Example: He was surprised the time **when he felt ill**.

An adverb clause acts as an adverb in a sentence – modifying a verb. Like an adverb, an adverb clause usually tells where, when, or how the action of the verb took place.

Example: **If you are late**, you may not get any dinner.

> Determine whether the noun or the verb is being modified.

Identify the italicized clauses by writing "adjective" or "adverb" in the spaces provided.

1. The boy *who won the race* was given an award. _____

2. On the hot days, they walked *where there was shade*. _____

3. *Because they tried very hard*, the students were rewarded. _____

4. The new school, *if it is possible*, will open next September. _____

5. He was a student *who always participated in extra-curricular activities*. _____

6. Their campsite was located *where they could easily get water*. _____

7. The reason *that he behaved that way* was not known. _____

8. The children knew *as soon as the bell sounded* that recess was over. _____

CHALLENGE

Create sentences using the adjective clause and the adverb clause below.

1. Adverb clause: after we had a swim in the lake

   _____

2. Adjective clause: where we grew up

   _____

A **Noun Clause** acts as a noun in a sentence and can function as a subject, direct object, predicate complement, or object of a preposition.

A. *Example (subject)*:

That she was the fastest runner was well-known.

"That she was the fastest runner" is the subject of the verb "was".

B. *Example (direct object)*:

She asked **where she could hang her coat**.

"Where she could hang her coat" is the direct object of the verb "asked" because it is what was being asked.

C. *Example (predicate complement)*:

The issue was **where they should schedule the game**.

"Where they should schedule the game" is complementing the sentence, following a form of the verb "to be".

D. *Example (object of a preposition)*:

They were hoping for **whomever could give them a lift** to arrive soon.

"Whomever could give them a lift" is the object of the preposition "for".

Underline the noun clause in each sentence below and state which type it is by indicating A, B, C, D (from the examples above) in the space provided.

1. She travelled to wherever nature could be enjoyed. _____

2. The problem was where they could park the car. _____

3. How we could settle the matter was our main concern. _____

4. That he could come up with the best idea won him the role of leader. _____

5. They were happy with whomever they had on their team. _____

6. The students asked when they would be dismissed. _____

CHALLENGE

Create sentences using the following noun clauses.

1. that she was my best friend

    _____

2. where the weather is hot

    _____

5 Verb Tenses

The **Progressive Tenses** refer to action that is ongoing.

Present Progressive: The action of the verb is ongoing in the present. Use "am, is, are" with the participle form of the verb.

Example: I **am playing** with my baby cousin.

Past Progressive: The action of the verb was ongoing in the past. Use "was/were" with the participle form of the verb.

Example: I **was playing** with my baby cousin yesterday.

Future Progressive: The action of the verb will be ongoing in the future. Use "will be" with the participle form of the verb.

Example: I **will be playing** with my cousin tomorrow.

I will be going to Edmonton with my family next Monday.

Use the verbs given to write sentences of your own in present progressive, past progressive, or future progressive tense.

1. study _____

2. eat _____

3. hide _____

4. give _____

Perfect Tenses

Present Perfect: It is used for action that began in the past, may have been finished at some time in the past, or continues into the present time. Use "has/have" with the participle form.

Example: I **have finished** my project, and she **has finished** hers, too.

Past Perfect: It is used for action that was completed in the past, or completed before some other action took place in the past. Use "had" with the participle form.

Example: I **had finished** my project before the teacher asked for it.

Future Perfect: It is used for action that will be completed some time in the future. Use "will have" with the participle form.

Example: By the time they come, I **will have finished the project**.

Exercise B

Complete the following sentences in present perfect, past perfect, or future perfect tense.

1. I don't think he _____ (read) that book before.

2. We _____ (tidy) up everything before the teacher came.

3. They _____ (make) the kite before next week's competition.

4. Nobody _____ (see) Marlene's painting yet.

5. After the opposing team _____ (score) twice, the coach finally called time-out.

6. By next Tuesday, I _____ (clear) up the backlog.

Perfect Progressive Tenses

Present Perfect Progressive: It is used for ongoing action that began in the past and is continuing into the future. Use "has/have been" with the participle form.

Example: They **have been playing** chess for almost four hours.

Past Perfect Progressive: It is used for continuous action in the past that occurred before another action or time in the past. Use "had been" with the participle form.

Example: I **had been playing** chess with Mary.

Future Perfect Progressive: It is used for continuous action that will have been completed in the future. Use "will have been" with the participle form.

Example: We **will have been playing** by the time she arrives.

Exercise C

State, in the space provided, the verb tense used in each of the sentences below.

1. Her mother had been a champion skater in her youth. _____

2. She was a student in our school. _____

3. He has been travelling through Europe. _____

4. We are members of the tennis club. _____

5. We will have been living in our house for three years this summer. _____

6. The time will come when the students go to a high school. _____

7. He is phoning his friend to come out to play. _____

8. It will have been four years since he moved here. _____

Transitive and Intransitive Verbs

Transitive verbs have direct objects. A direct object receives the action of the verb.

Examples: He lifted the box onto the table.

"Lifted" is a transitive verb because it passes the action of lifting to the direct object "box".

He felt shy around the strangers.

"Felt" is an intransitive verb because it does not pass on its action to a direct object.

Underline the verbs in the sentences below and state whether they are transitive (TR) or intransitive (INT).

1. His father finally caught a fish after three hours on the lake. _____

2. She thought about quitting the swim team. _____

3. They built a skating rink in the backyard. _____

4. The kite blew away in the wind. _____

5. They competed in the contest but didn't win. _____

6. They rented a boat for fishing. _____

7. The fire alarm sounded and we all left the building. _____

8. The children go for a long hike in the woods. _____

9. The baby cried loudly but nobody heard him. _____

10. Mark shot the puck right into the goal. _____

> Many verbs can be either transitive or intransitive, depending on how they are used.

Exercise E

Use the appropriate form of the verbs to write sentences of your own and state whether they are transitive (TR) or intransitive (INT).

1. taste _____ (   )

2. hurt _____ (   )

3. rise _____ (   )

4. blow _____ (   )

5. play _____ (   )

6. fly _____ (   )

Problem Verbs

The following pairs of verbs cause problems because they sound similar and have similar meanings.

In each pair, one verb is transitive, which means it takes a direct object.

Base word	Past	Past Participle	Present Participle
lie	lay	lain	lying
lay	laid	laid	laying
sit	sat	sat	sitting
set	set	set	setting
rise	rose	risen	rising
raise	raised	raised	raising

Exercise 7

Use the correct form of the words from the chart in each of the sentences below.

1. He _____ (rose, raised) from the bed still tired.

2. The maid is _____ (lying, laying) the table cloth on the table.

3. Can you see the cat _____ (lying, laying) under the table?

4. She _____ (sat, set) the tray in her lap.

5. The little boy was _____ (sitting, setting) quietly waiting for his turn.

6. She _____ (raised, rose) herself into an upright position.

7. The price of food is _____ (rising, raising).

8. The grocer will _____ (raise, rise) the price of food.

9. The teacher _____ (lay, laid) the books on the desk.

10. She _____ (laid, lay) on the carpet reading her book.

6 Verbals and Verbal Phrases

 **Verbals** are words that are formed from verbs but function as nouns, adjectives, or adverbs in a sentence. There are three types of verbals: gerunds, participles, and infinitives.

Present and Past Participles

The Present Participle is the "ing" form of a verb. The Past Participle form of most verbs is formed by adding "ed". Some verbs have irregular past participle forms, e.g. "be" becomes "been", "see" becomes "seen", and "hide" becomes "hidden".

Exercise A

Underline the present or past participle(s) in each sentence and state whether it is an adjective (ADJ) or an adverb (ADV).

1. The dreaming princess awoke startled. _____ _____

2. The pirates searched for the hidden treasure. _____

3. The defeated team left the playing field first. _____ _____

4. The barbecued hamburgers were delicious. _____

5. His torn jacket needed repair. _____

6. The opening song was the one they had rehearsed. _____

7. The swinging chair was placed on the old front porch. _____

 **Participle Phrases**

Present Participle: Standing on the street corner, Ken waited for his friends.

The present participle phrase acts as an adjective modifying "Ken".

Past Participle: Stuck in the traffic jam, Ken's friends were going to be late.

The past participle phrase acts as an adjective modifying "Ken's friends".

Exercise B

Create sentences using the participle phrases given.

1. fishing in the lake

_____

2. cheering loudly

_____

3. hidden from their sight

_____

4. worried that they would be late

_____

5. tired of waiting

_____

A **Gerund** is a verbal that ends in "ing" and is used as a noun in a sentence.

It may appear as the subject of a sentence, as a direct object of a verb, or as the object of a preposition.

Examples: **Skiing** is a winter sport. (subject of the verb "is")
She likes **skiing** as a winter sport. (direct object of the verb "likes")
She was tired of **skiing**. (object of the preposition "of")

Exercise C

A verb or preposition is suggested, but you may choose your own.

Use each gerund given in a sentence as the part of speech indicated.

1. laughing – subject of the verb "make"

_____

2. flying – subject of the verb "is"

_____

3. swimming – object of the verb "tried"

_____

4. sleeping – object of the preposition "for"

_____

5. running – subject of the verb "is"

_____

6. falling – object of the preposition "of"

_____

A **Gerund Phrase** consists of a gerund, its modifiers, its objects, and its complements.
Example: **Batting better than the other players** was his main goal.

Exercise D

Create sentences using the following gerund phrases.

> Remember: A gerund phrase acts as a noun — subject, object, or object of a preposition.

1. making chocolate chip cookies

    _____

2. hoping for good weather

    _____

3. skating on the frozen river

    _____

4. listening to music

    _____

5. getting good grades

    _____

CHALLENGE

Make use of the following participles as adjectives or adverbs to compose a meaningful paragraph.

exciting	competing	excited	broken	exhausted

_____

_____

_____

_____

_____

An **Infinitive** is a verbal that begins with the word "to" such as "to be", "to go", and "to say".

An infinitive can function as a noun, adjective, or adverb in a sentence.

Example: She likes **to ride** her bicycle. (noun – object)
She gave her brother a turn **to ride** her bicycle. (adjective)
She was prepared **to ride** her bicycle. (adverb)

Exercise E

State the type of use (noun, adjective, adverb) for each infinitive below.

1. *To rest* is necessary after a strenuous workout.   _____

2. He returned home *to eat*.   _____

3. He was ready *to play*.   _____

4. She wanted *to write* a letter.   _____

5. *To sing* well is a rare talent.   _____

6. He wanted *to quit* the team.

An **Infinitive Phrase** consists of an infinitive, its modifier, and any complements.
Example: **To be a successful student** is what he worked for.

Exercise F

Create sentences from the infinitive phrases below.

1. to run in a race

    _____

2. to end the school year

    _____

3. to be a good neighbour

    _____

4. to eat in a restaurant

    _____

5. to play against a strong team

    _____

7 Direct and Indirect (Reported) Speech

Direct Speech repeats exact words spoken; these words are put in between quotation marks.

Example: Janet said, "I like the red dress."

Indirect Speech is usually used to report what someone else said, and no quotation marks are needed.

Example: Janet said that she liked the red dress.

To change direct speech to indirect speech involves tense changes. Usually, the tense in indirect speech is **one tense back in time** from that in direct speech.

Exercise A

Change the following to indirect speech.

> You don't need to change the tense if the reporting verb is in the present, or if the statement is about something that is still true.

1. "I enjoy a walk in the park," he said.

   _____

2. She said, "I am preparing for the test."

   _____

3. Simon explained, "I missed the school bus."

   _____

4. "Peter had just gone out," Brian said.

   _____

5. They explained, "We were busy writing the report."

   _____

6. Fiona said, "There are now three territories in Canada."

   _____

7. The teacher said, "I'll be away most of the week."

   _____

8. "I've done all my work," Marilyn said.

   _____

9. "We have been waiting for Helen," the girls said.

   _____

10. Nicole says, "I'm never good at swimming."

   _____

Change of Time Reference

In indirect speech, we need to change time reference.

Example: "We will go to Chicago **tomorrow**," Brian said.
Brian said that they would go to Chicago **the next day**.

Change of Personal Pronouns

We need to change personal pronouns to the third person singular or plural, except when the speaker reports his own words.

I / me / my / mine / you / your / yours → him / his / her / hers
we / us / our / ours / you / your / yours → they / their / theirs

Example: Nolan said to her, "**I** like the way **you** dance."
Nolan told her that **he** liked the way **she** danced.

Exercise B

Change the following sentences to indirect speech using the proper time reference.

that day   the day before   two days before
a week before   the following week
the previous week   that week   two days later

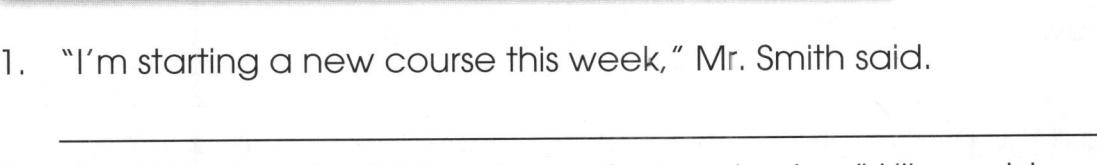

Choose from these time references.

1. "I'm starting a new course this week," Mr. Smith said.

_____

2. "I went to the dentist the day before yesterday," Lilian said.

_____

3. "The players stayed at that hotel last week," he told us.

_____

4. He said, "Next week, there will be two new boys joining us."

_____

5. The teacher said, "John was absent today."

_____

6. Ben said, "I saw John yesterday in the movie theatre."

_____

7. "The accident happened a week ago," said the police officer.

_____

8. "My cousin will come the day after tomorrow," said Julie.

_____

Indirect Questions

Normal word order, with the necessary tense change, is used in indirect questions, and there is no need to use "do", "does" or "did".

Example: Helen asked her mother, "Which one did you choose?"
Helen asked her mother which one **she had chosen**.

Change Yes / No questions to indirect questions by using "ask" + if / whether.

Example: The old man asked, "Is it snowing?"
The old man **asked if it was snowing**.

Change the following questions to indirect speech.

1. "How do we get there?" asked the children.

   _____

2. She asked me, "Have you been to Cambridge before?"

   _____

3. "Have you got a CD player?" Shannon asked.

   _____

4. "Did you draw the picture?" the teacher asked Shawn.

   _____

5. "Can you use the programme?" the manager asked the applicant.

   _____

6. The girls asked, "When can we go in?"

   _____

CHALLENGE

Report what Brad says using indirect speech.

I ran into Gord last week. When he saw me, he said, "We're having a practice session after school. Do you want to join us?" I replied, "I won't be joining you because I haven't completed my science project."

_____

_____

_____

Change the following indirect statements to direct ones.

1. The captain told them that the game would be postponed to the following Friday.

    _____

2. I asked if we had to pay for the trip.

    _____

3. She remarked that the test was too difficult for the average students.

    _____

4. She told him that she liked his new suit.

    _____

5. The driver said that he had been waiting there for more than an hour.

    _____

6. She asked me what time I would be home.

    _____

Exercise E

Correct the following indirect statements.

1. The teacher asked the new boy what is his name.

    _____

2. I explained that plants needed water, light, and earth to grow.

    _____

3. She said she met John last month.

    _____

4. Simon said that he has never been to Disneyland.

    _____

5. The teacher asked us if anyone of us wants to stay behind.

    _____

6. The police officer asked me did I see a tall man with a brown briefcase.

    _____

Progress Test 1

The Sentence and Its Parts

Exercise A

Decide whether each sentence expresses a complete thought. Place the letter "C" for complete and "Inc" for incomplete after each sentence in the space provided.

1. Unless he was asked to go. _____
2. During the weekend. _____
3. Little wonder I didn't realize that! _____
4. The day went by so quickly. _____
5. Look out! _____
6. Instead of giving the prize to the winning student. _____
7. You'd better be careful. _____
8. Against the strong wind, he trudged along. _____
9. Don't you know the answer? _____

> Sentences must express a complete thought.

Exercise B

Add your own words to turn the following incomplete sentences into complete ones.

1. If our teacher is free, _____
2. Whenever we want to play baseball, _____
3. The children in the schoolyard _____
4. When the guests arrived, _____
5. A leisurely walk through the woods _____
6. Although the party was over, _____
7. Apart from reading the notes, _____
8. No matter how hard he tried, _____
9. Before the game began, _____
10. Against the strong wind and the heavy snow, _____
_____

Direct and Indirect Objects

A direct object is the receiver of the action of the verb; an indirect object is one to whom or what the action of the verb is directed.

Exercise C

Underline the objects and state whether they are direct or indirect.

Only indicate objects of the verbs; do not indicate objects of the prepositions.

1. They ate sandwiches for lunch. _____
2. She gave him a gift for his birthday. _____ _____
3. The teacher handed her the books to be distributed. _____ _____
4. He asked her a question that she could not answer. _____ _____
5. Nobody knows the answer to the question. _____
6. He told us a scary story at the camp before going to bed. _____ _____

Nouns

Exercise D

Form compound nouns by connecting the words that match.

Column A	Column B	New Word
1. grand	room	1. _____
2. text	father	2. _____
3. high	works	3. _____
4. floppy	in-law	4. _____
5. living	book	5. _____
6. fire	slide	6. _____
7. mother	school	7. _____
8. water	disk	8. _____

Progress Test 1

Exercise E

Identify each noun as either "Common", "Proper", "Concrete", or "Abstract". Place the description in the space provided.

1. Mr. Johnson _____   2. student _____
3. Calgary _____   4. love _____
5. anger _____   6. Ford _____
7. automobile _____   8. joy _____
9. music _____   10. explosion _____

Noun Plurals

Exercise F

Place the plural forms of the nouns below in the space provided.

1. proof _____   2. patio _____
3. tomato _____   4. elf _____
5. chief _____   6. canoe _____
7. hero _____   8. man _____
9. moose _____   10. pants _____
11. scissors _____   12. sky _____

Pronouns

Exercise G

Convert the subjective pronouns to objective and possessive forms.

Subjective	Objective	Possessive
1. I	_____	_____
2. We	_____	_____
3. They	_____	_____
4. He	_____	_____
5. She	_____	_____
6. It	_____	_____

Relative Pronouns

Exercise H

Underline the relative pronoun that connects to a noun in each sentence below.

1. The person who was supposed to open the school was late.
2. He bought the car that best suited his needs.
3. The class which occupied the new classroom was made up of both grades.
4. The student to whom the teacher is talking is my brother.
5. We went to the restaurant where there was a salad bar.

Adverb and Adjective Phrases

Exercise I

Underline the adjective phrases and put the adverb phrases in parentheses ( ).

1. In the heat of the day, they went for a swim.
2. The boys of the sixth grade played in the yard.
3. During the night, the dog in the yard barked endlessly.

Descriptors - Comparative and Superlative

Exercise J

Use auxiliary (helping) words where necessary.

Write the comparative and superlative forms of the regular descriptors below.

Regular	Comparative	Superlative
1. good	_____	_____
2. much	_____	_____
3. well	_____	_____
4. far	_____	_____
5. bold	_____	_____
6. bad	_____	_____

Progress Test 1

Clauses

Exercise K

Underline the dependent clauses in the sentences below.

1. Because he won the race, he was given a trophy.

2. She arrived on time although she left late.

3. Whenever we get together, we have a good time.

4. He fell asleep when the teacher was writing on the chalkboard.

5. Unless you come on time, you will not be allowed in.

Verb Tenses

Exercise L

Fill in the blanks with the correct form of the verbs in parentheses.

Dad and Uncle Fred 1._____ (play) tennis since eight o'clock and it 2._____ (seem) like they 3._____ (continue) to play until noon. They 4._____ (enjoy) the game very much even though neither of them 5._____ (be) really that good at it. Dad 6._____ (promise) to take me to the Railroad Restaurant for lunch. In fact, he 7._____ (make) a reservation already. We 8._____ (have) lunch in one of the train compartments.

Transitive and Intransitive Verbs

Exercise M

State whether the italicized verbs are transitive or intransitive.

1. She *walked* her dog in the park.   _____

2. He *liked* a walk in the park in the morning.   _____

3. She *was* too shy to make a speech in front of the class. _____

4. The rope *held* the boat close to the dock. _____

5. The little girl *laughed* happily. _____

Verbals

Exercise N

There may be more than one verbal in each sentence. Verbals can be nouns, adjectives, or adverbs.

Underline the verbal(s) in each sentence below.

1. Running is good exercise but there are also hidden benefits.
2. He was bitten by a mosquito and his arm was swelling.
3. Feeling much better, he returned to school.
4. The chosen students represented the school in the debating contest.
5. He preferred eating at home.
6. To help is better than to hinder.

Direct and Indirect Speech

Exercise O

Change the following from direct to indirect speech.

1. Kitty asked Paul, "Do you think I can make the team?"

   _____

2. The bus driver said, "We'll be leaving at two."

   _____

3. "Where should I go for help?" the little boy asked.

   _____

4. "Is she the one who sang in our concert last year?" Betsy asked.

   _____

5. I explained, "The CPU is the brain of the computer."

   _____

8 Building Sentences

Sentence Combining

Too many short sentences in a paragraph can be boring for the reader.

Example(1):   John has a dog. The dog is a Collie. The dog's name is Rufus.
Better: John's dog, Rufus, is a Collie.   or   John has a Collie dog named Rufus.

Example(2):   It was raining. The game ended. We all got wet.
Better: Because it was raining, the game ended and we all got wet.
                  "Because it was raining" is a dependent clause attached to the compound sentence "the game ended and we all got wet."

To combine short sentences into a longer sentence, you may have to do one of the following:
a. change a short sentence to a single word adjective
b. make one of the sentences a dependent clause
c. create a compound sentence

Combine each of the following groups of sentences into one sentence.

1. The children played. They played in the yard. They played soccer.

    _____

2. He arrived here. He arrived late. The bus was delayed.

    _____

3. They went on holiday. They went to Florida. They went during the summer.

    _____

4. Randall is Lauren's brother. He is 19 years old. He attends university.

    _____

5. Kara is a dancer. Kara makes up her own dances. Kara is creative.

    _____

6. The dog chased the ball. The ball went into the water. The dog went into the water, too.

    _____

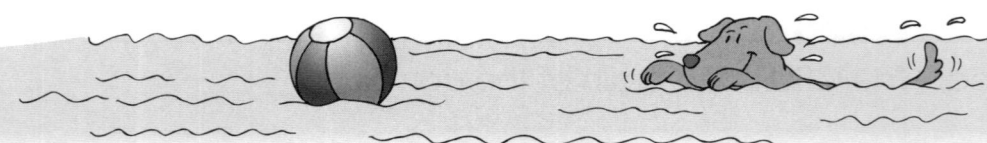

Problem Sentences

Run-On Sentences

A run-on sentence is formed when two or more independent clauses (sentences) are placed together as one sentence without connecting words.

Example: Peter's brother is in grade seven he goes to the same school.
Correction(1): Peter's brother is in grade seven and he goes to the same school.
Correction(2): Peter's brother, who is in grade seven, goes to the same school.

To repair a run-on sentence, do one of the following:
a. use a conjunction
b. create two sentences
c. change one independent clause to a dependent clause
d. use a semicolon between the two independent clauses

Exercise B

> Use connecting words such as "because", "and", "when", "as", and "after".

Correct the following run-on sentences.

1. He was the fastest runner he won every race.

    _____

2. The game was over everyone went home.

    _____

3. The bell sounded the race was on.

    _____

4. It rained heavily we ran for shelter.

    _____

5. Richard had the lead role in the school play he played a prince.

    _____

6. The school parent committee organized a fundraising campaign they needed money for sports equipment.

    _____

7. In the morning they met at the bus stop they took the 8 o'clock bus.

    _____

8. The highway was closed the potholes needed repair.

    _____

9. My dog is cute it was my birthday present.

    _____

A **Comma Splice** occurs when two independent clauses are separated by a comma.

Example: The game went into overtime, the teams took a quick rest.
The sentence does not have a connecting word linking the two independent clauses.

Correction: When the game went into overtime, the teams took a quick rest.
In this sentence, the independent clause "the game went into overtime" becomes a dependent clause with the connecting word "when".

Exercise C

Correct the comma splice in each sentence below.

To repair a comma splice error, you might use one of the following suggestions:
a. change one independent clause to a dependent clause
b. use a conjunction to join the two independent clauses
c. create two sentences

1. The windows were opened, the night was very warm.

   _____

2. The dog barked, there was someone at the door.

   _____

3. Nightfall came, the moon shone brightly.

   _____

4. After the rain, a rainbow appeared in the sky, it was a beautiful sight.

   _____

5. The teacher asked everyone to be quiet, there was silence in the room.

   _____

6. It was her 80th birthday party, it was a very special event.

   _____

7. The car came to a screeching halt, it just missed hitting the pedestrian.

   _____

8. The children heard strange noise in the dark house, they rushed out screamimg.

   _____

The following paragraph contains a series of short sentences that can be combined into compound or complex sentences. Make the necessary corrections and rewrite the paragraph in the space provided.

Avoid repeating words; group sentences that have a common topic, and then combine them.

The City of Toronto

Toronto is a big city. It is located in the province of Ontario. It is situated on Lake Ontario. Toronto is the largest city in Canada. The population of Toronto is nearly 3,000,000. Toronto has many theatres. Toronto is the third largest live theatre centre in the world. New York City is the largest live theatre centre in the world. London, England is the second largest live theatre centre in the world. Toronto has many professional sports teams. Toronto has a professional baseball team. The name of the professional baseball team in Toronto is the Toronto Blue Jays. Toronto has a professional basketball team. The name of the basketball team is the Toronto Raptors. Toronto has a professional hockey team. The name of the hockey team is the Toronto Maple Leafs. Toronto has a new arena. The name of the new arena is the Air Canada Centre. The Raptors and the Leafs play in the Air Canada Centre.

_____

_____

_____

_____

_____

_____

_____

_____

_____

_____

9 The Comma, the Colon, and the Semicolon

The Comma

Commas are used to:

A. separate words or phrases in a series.

Example: When the sun comes up, the dew melts, and the birds sing, we know morning has arrived.

B. separate adjectives before a noun when the adjectives are independent modifiers of the noun.

Example: The red car was parked in front of the large, elegant home.

C. separate pairs of words in a series.

Example: Players and coaches, and parents and fans filled the arena.

D. separate a dependent clause from an independent clause when the dependent clause appears first in the sentence.

Example: Although he was new to the school, he made many friends.
But there is no comma when the independent clause appears first:
He made many friends although he was new to the school.

E. set off words in apposition.

Example: My teacher, Miss Johnson, lives in our neighbourhood.

F. set off words, phrases, or clauses that are in contrast.

Example: Students should be hardworking, not lazy.

G. set off transitional words such as "nevertheless", "moreover", "indeed", and "of course".

Example: Nevertheless, once we set the rules, the games went smoothly.

H. set off a direct quotation.

Examples: She stated, "This is the best dinner I have ever had."
"It is early," he said. "We have much work to do."

Insert commas where needed.

The number in parentheses indicates the number of commas needed for each sentence.

1. She was born on July 22 1990. (1)

2. They planted tomatoes cucumbers radishes and lettuce in their backyard. (3)

3. Laughing not crying is the preferred reaction. (2)

4. Indeed the need for hard work is something we all understand. (1)

5. He bought a shiny new bicycle which he rode to school. (1)

6. When they arrived at our house we gave them a warm welcome. (1)

7. "We can be successful" she proclaimed "if we work hard." (2)

8. You must drive in this direction not the other way round. (1)

Commas for Non-Restrictive Adjective Clauses

A non-restrictive adjective clause is one that is not necessary in a sentence to clarify meaning.

Example: My friend, **whom I have known for a long time**, plays on my hockey team.
A non-restrictive adjective clause is set off by commas from the noun it describes.

A restrictive adjective clause is one where the information is essential to defining the noun described.

Example: We keep our equipment **that we use for most sports** locked in the basement.
There is no comma used in this case as the clause is essential to describing the equipment.

Exercise B

Decide whether each sentence below contains a non-restrictive or a restrictive adjective clause, and add commas as needed.

1. The car *that we purchased* was not brand new. _____
2. The people *who paid their money* were guaranteed good seats. _____
3. The show *which originated in another city* was scheduled to begin next week. _____
4. The team captain *who was selected by a team vote* represented us very well. _____
5. The day *that he remembers best* was the day that his sister was born. _____
6. Mr. Randall was a teacher *whom we all admired*. _____

Nouns in Apposition

Apposition refers to a description of a noun that is set off and parallel to the noun it describes.

Example: My uncle, **Professor Jones**, works at a university.

Exercise C

Check the sentences with correct use of commas.

1. My dog, Abbey, loves to chase a ball. _____
2. John the new team member scored the winning goal. _____
3. The visitor, a tall, heavy man told interesting stories. _____
4. They shopped at a store, a local supermarket, for all their groceries. _____
5. I don't think Mr. Jones, our teacher will go with us. _____
6. Jenny's cousin Jeremy has won the crossword puzzle contest. _____
7. There is a tall man, a Mr Jones, waiting outside to see you. _____

The Colon

A colon is used:

A. to introduce items in a series.
   Example: They baked the following foods: cookies, bread, bagels, and cakes.

B. to introduce a statement or formal quotation.
   Example: His school had one main goal: all students would succeed.

C. between independent clauses when one clause finishes the idea of the first.
   Example: Sports was more than recreation to him: it was his life.

D. to set off an appositive; it is often used with "specifically", "that is", "namely", or "in other words".
   Example: She has one favourite activity: namely, horseback riding.

E. after a formal greeting in a letter.
   Example: Dear Mr. Smith:

F. between hours and minutes when stating precise time.
   Example: 4:33 a.m.

G. to set off a subtitle from the main title.
   Example: He read the newspaper article "World Travel: Great Escapes".

Exercise D

Insert a colon into each of the following sentences.

1. Today we purchased many items for the party balloons, cakes, and soft drinks.

2. He wanted only one gift a watch.

3. The children had no recess the rain was too intense.

4. The rule is stated clearly "Never touch the ball with your hands."

5. When she moved away, it was a sad day that was the only home she knew.

6. The bag was filled with treats chips, cookies, candy bars, and liquorice.

7. He was upset at losing the game in other words, he was very disappointed.

8. After all her effort in preparing for the race, only one thing mattered being there.

9. She has been dreaming of visiting a place Disneyland.

The Semicolon

A semicolon is used to join two sentences (independent clauses) that are closely related in topic.

By using a semicolon, we can avoid run-on sentences.

Example: The teacher asked the questions; the students gave the answers.

Exercise E

Choose the best pairings of independent clauses below and join them with a semicolon.

1. The referee blew his whistle
2. Children lined up to go swimming
3. Summer holidays are a time for travel
4. Worrying will do no good
5. We visited Canada's Wonderland
6. They learned about pioneers
7. The playground was covered in snow

- we may go to British Columbia
- we spent the entire day going on rides
- they were interested in the hardships they faced
- cction is needed
- there had been a big storm overnight
- the pool had not yet opened
- the game came to a halt

1. _____
2. _____
3. _____
4. _____
5. _____
6. _____
7. _____

CHALLENGE

Examine the use of colons and semicolons in the sentences below and write "C" for correct or "I" for incorrect at the end of each sentence.

1. They watched the game from the stands; which gave them a ____
   great view. ____
2. We ate dinner in a restaurant; the food was delicious. ____
3. It all came down to one thing: courage. ____
4. The final day of the school year arrived; the students were excited. ____
5. Some of the positions were: goalie, defence, forward, and centre.
6. We walked along the river's edge: ducks swam alongside us. ____

10 Dashes, Hyphens, Brackets, and Parentheses

The Dash

Use a dash to:

1. separate a series at the beginning of a sentence from the explanatory section of the sentence.

   Example: A positive attitude, a will to work hard, and the desire to win – these are the traits of a champion.

   Notice that the above sentence begins with a series of things, and is followed by an explanation of what those things are.

2. set off a parenthetical description. A parenthetical description is an explanation or a comment to further the reader's understanding of the sentence.

   Example: The final play-off game – the best game of the year – was played on home ice.

   The words "the best game of the year" is parenthetical because it adds further information in the middle of the sentence to the noun "game".

3. set off at the end of a sentence a further explanation of an idea.

   Example: They were determined to achieve on goal – victory.

Exercise A

Copy the following sentences placing dashes where needed. Refer to the examples above.

1. The summer cottage the one situated on an island was our favourite summer place.

   _____

2. When the sun went down, we were left with one thing darkness.

   _____

3. The crashing waves, the howling wind, and the huge rocks all spelled one thing danger.

   _____

4. Computers, digital cameras, palm pilots, and cell phones these are the new electronic toys.

   _____

5. The main idea of the story the fact that a young girl had to go away to a private school made it interesting for children to read.

   _____

The Hyphen

A hyphen is used to join compound words, to divide a word into syllables, and to indicate a split in a word at the end of a line.

A. **Compound Adjectives**: hyphenate two words that act as a single adjective.

Examples: a well-known person; a law-school graduate

B. **Compound Numbers and Fractions**: use a hyphen to connect numbers that are spelled out and to connect fractions used as adjectives. Do not hyphenate fractions used as nouns.

Examples: **twenty-one years old**; **one-fifth more**; but no hyphen for: **one half of the country**

C. **Prefixes and Suffixes**: normally a hyphen is not used between a prefix or suffix and the root word. There are, however, a number of exceptions. Usually, using a hyphen prevents confusion of meaning.

Example: She will **re-create** the masterpiece painting.   but
Painting, to her, is a form of **recreation**.

The first sentence shows the need for a hyphen to define the word and avoid confusing it with the similar word in the second sentence.

Also, use a hyphen between a prefix and its root if the root word is capitalized.

Examples: semi-industrial, anti-European

Copy the sentences below adding hyphens where necessary.

1. The under six year olds can play in the ball room.

   _____

2. The other children are divided into players and non players.

   _____

3. They had to recount the money because someone demanded a re count.

   _____

4. She lived in a coop apartment that had a chicken coop in the back.

   _____

5. Over one half of the voters supported the pro economy candidate.

   _____

6. He drove a semi automatic tractor to do one third of the ploughing.

   _____

7. He was only thirty two when he became vice president in charge of over two thirds of the company.

   _____

Brackets are used most often in formal writing such as essays, periodicals, newspaper articles, and journals.

The purpose of brackets is to add additional material into a statement.

Example: "This explorer **[Champlain]** started a settlement at what is now known as Quebec City."

The word "Champlain" is inserted into the quotation and must be shown as an addition to the actual statement being quoted. Notice that without this insert, the sentence is complete on its own.

Exercise C

In the following statements, insert brackets [ ] where necessary.

1. The message read: "Wayne Gretsky hockey great will be in charge of forming the Canadian World Junior Team."

2. He proclaimed, "The World Junior Hockey Tournament many hockey fans consider the best hockey entertainment is fast becoming popular worldwide."

3. He announced, "The company president Mr. Forsythe will address the Board of Directors."

4. The year of Canada's Confederation 1867 was one hundred years before Expo in Montreal.

Parentheses

One main difference between the use of **parentheses** and the use of **dashes** is that parentheses enclose secondary information while dashes are used to emphasize a statement within a sentence.

Parentheses are used to enclose additional information that may not be essential to the understanding of the sentence but may be useful to know. Parentheses may also be used to add a comment to a statement.

Example (1): The neighbourhood (a very tidy, little area) was located on the park.

Example (2): Prince Edward Island is an island (see map) across from Nova Scotia.

Parentheses are also used to show letters and numbers that designate items in a series.

Example (1): Before leaving for your trip you should (a) check your luggage (b) make sure you have your tickets and passport, and (c) confirm the time of your flight.

Example (2): He wanted to get (1) a new bicycle (2) new riding gear, and (3) a map of riding trails.

Exercise D

Place parentheses where needed in the sentences below.

1. The students in this school of which I am one will organize a fundraising campaign.

2. The purchase of new band uniforms once the money is given will make a big difference.

3. The Grey Cup a Canadian ritual is played in a different city each year.

4. The plan was to 1 hold a meeting 2 choose a leader, and 3 divide up the duties.

5. Follow the road 8 km to the corner store and turn left.

6. My idea the plan to create a special group to raise money for the hospital requires the involvement from my friends.

7. The new student his name is Jordan sits next to me.

Other Structural Devices

Ellipsis Dots are used to indicate that a part of a quotation is missing. In some cases, a quotation may be longer than the information needed from it; therefore, ellipses are used to shorten the quotation.

Example: The teacher asked, "Please empty your desk because the custodians will be coming... before next Friday."

Exercise E

Read each quotation below and decide where ellipsis dots should be inserted. Copy the sentences with your inserted ellipsis dots.

> If the statement seems complete, the ellipses must come at the end.

1. "There are many types of insects including which are found mainly in the Rain Forest."

   _____

   _____

2. "The importance of regular fitness cannot be underestimated since."

   _____

3. "When we take matters into our own hands these are the main issues."

   _____

4. "The difference in learning styles can be profound."

   _____

5. "The flight across took more than three hours and twenty minutes."

   _____

11 Varying Sentence Construction

Using Phrases to Begin a Sentence

Varying the construction of sentences makes for a more interesting reading experience. Using prepositional, verbal, and infinitive phrases can provide a variety of ways to construct sentences.

Using prepositional phrases:

Example: We went fishing under the bridge.   becomes
Under the bridge, we went fishing.

Using verbal phrases:

Example: He wore a blue coat to the game.   becomes
Wearing a blue coat, he went to the game.

Using gerunds:

Example: One of her favourite activities is singing.   becomes
Singing is one of her favourite activities.

Using infinitive phrases:

Example: You must practise to qualify for the team.   becomes
To qualify for the team, you must practise.

Exercise A

Practise making sentences more interesting by changing the construction. You may have to change verb forms to suit the changes. Be creative, but maintain the essence of the sentence meaning.

1. He wanted to be first in his class in Science and Mathematics.

    To be first _____

2. She wore her best clothes when she went to the party.

    Wearing _____

3. Being a professional athlete would be a wonderful career.

    To be _____

4. We walked down to the lakefront and met our friends.

    Walking _____

5. The class gathered in the park for an outdoor class.

    Gathering _____

6. He fell off his bicycle and injured his arm.

    Having _____

Inverting Word Order

The usual order of words in a sentence is subject-verb-object. Inverting the order of words in a sentence can create an interesting presentation of ideas.

Example: The birds flew in unison across the night sky.   becomes

In unison across the night sky flew the birds.   or

Across the night sky, the birds flew in unison.

Exercise B

Invert the order of words in each sentence below to form new ways of presenting the idea. Be sure to use commas where necessary.

1. The teacher, the one who was new to the school, could not find his classroom.

   _____

2. In the early morning, the dew frosted the windshields of the cars.

   _____

3. The students assembled in the library to hear the speeches.

   _____

4. During the rainfall, we found shelter under the canopy.

   _____

5. Baseball, basketball, hockey, and football were the sports he liked to play at school.

   _____

6. He spoke softly whenever he was working in the library.

   _____

7. The game being tied at the buzzer was sent into overtime.

   _____

8. We walked for miles through the forest before reaching the campsite near the river.

   _____

Write the following sentence in two different ways. The beginnings are given.

If you enjoy writing stories, you should always take time to express your creativity.

1. You _____

2. Time _____

Building Detailed Sentences

Adding details and descriptive language can form interesting sentences.

Example (1): I walked down the street.
Walking down the long narrow street, I felt a cool gush of wind.

The street has been described and additional information has been added to enhance the reader's experience.

Example (2): Hockey is a favourite Canadian sport.
Hockey, Canada's favourite sport, is enjoyed by athletes of all ages.

In this example, the words "Canada's favourite sport" have been placed in apposition to the noun "Hockey". Additional information has also been added to enrich the sentence.

Exercise C

Expand the following sentences by adding descriptive details. You might also convert a verb to a verbal, create a subordinate clause, or add adjective and adverb phrases to create interesting detailed sentences.

> You may change the subject or the verb and add objects to create more vivid sentences. Refer to the examples above.

1. The children played in the schoolyard.

   _____

2. The moon rose in the night sky.

   _____

3. We listened to songs on the radio.

   _____

4. They went on vacation.

   _____

5. We took the subway downtown.

   _____

6. There were great bargains at the garage sale.

   _____

7. Autumn is a nice time of the year.

   _____

8. The snow fell on the city.

   _____

9. The sailboat floated along.

   _____

10. They rode their bicycles.

    _____

11. The children looked for a birthday gift.

    _____

12. We watched TV.

    _____

CHALLENGE

Expand the girl's sentence in three different ways.

1. _____

   _____

2. _____

   _____

3. _____

   _____

The boys were exhausted.

12 Paragraph Construction

The Paragraph

A **Paragraph** is made up of a group of sentences with a common topic.

The **Topic Sentence** is the first sentence of a paragraph. It states or suggests the main idea of the paragraph.

A paragraph must have **unity** and **coherence**. When a paragraph has unity, all its sentences relate to a single idea. Coherence refers to the logical sequence in which the sentences are arranged in a paragraph.

Exercise A

In each group of sentences below, place the number 1 beside the topic sentence. Place the numbers 2,3, and 4 to indicate the order in which the next sentences should appear to make a coherent paragraph.

A. Michael is also a very unselfish player; he is always setting up other players to score goals. _____

Without Michael on our team, we would not be in first place in the league. _____

Michael is the best hockey player on the team. _____

He has scored more goals than any of his team-mates this season. _____

B. When the holiday is over, we are always sad to leave. _____

Every year, we rent a cottage on Georgian Bay for the month of July. _____

Our cottage is equipped with a boat for water-skiing and a large dock for swimming. _____

Georgian Bay is less than a three-hour drive from our home in Toronto. _____

C. His cousins were very bright and learned basic English very quickly. _____

Enzo's cousins from Italy arrived to spend the summer in Canada. _____

When their holiday was over, they could express themselves very well. _____

They did not speak a word of English so Enzo began to teach them some everyday expressions. _____

Exercise B

Write a topic sentence for each short paragraph below. Make sure that your topic sentence introduces the main idea of the sentences in the paragraph.

1. Topic sentence: _____
   _____

   We boarded the bus at 8:00 a.m. because the trip was going to take two hours. When we arrived at the ski hills, we rushed into the chalet to get our equipment. Within half an hour, we were zooming down the ski hills.

2. Topic sentence: _____
   _____

   We drove to the airport three hours before the scheduled time of our departure. Once we got checked in, we had to find a way to spend the next two hours. My parents went to the bookstore while I played a few video games. Finally, we got the call to board, and suddenly I became very excited.

3. Topic sentence: _____
   _____

   All the students sat waiting for the teacher to draw the name of the winner. He shuffled the tickets once, twice, and then he finally reached into the hat and pulled out a name. First he stated that the winner was a girl; then he indicated which row of seats she sat in. We were waiting in anticipation when he finally made the announcement.

4. Topic sentence: _____
   _____

   We decided to make a special birthday card instead of buying one. My brother is a very good artist so he drew the pictures. My job was to write the message. When we gave our mother the card, she was delighted.

Expanding the Topic Sentence

A topic sentence should be detailed and specific enough to be easily developed further in the sentences that follow.

Examples:

Broad topic sentence: Playing sports is fun.
Specific topic sentence: Playing sports can be a great way to get fit.

Broad topic sentence: The summer holidays will soon be here.
Specific topic sentence: When the summer holidays arrive, we will leave for our vacation in British Columbia.

Exercise C

Write an expanded topic sentence for each broad topic sentence below. Use specific details to make your topic sentence more precise than the one given.

1. Snowboarding is fun.

    Revised: _When you go rushing down the hill_

2. We watched a horror movie.

    Revised: _and, we could not go to sleep the next night_

3. The race began.

    Revised: _Summy was in fist and her won_

4. The weather was stormy.

    Revised: _and windy no one dared to go outside_

5. We went for a sail on his new boat.

    Revised: _for two good hours then we got sea sick_

6. The live performance was exciting.

    Revised: _because my cousin was the lead singer_

7. The Beatles sold millions of records.

    Revised: _and got millions of dollars_

8. Watching too much television can be a waste of time.

    Revised: _because thres nothing good to watch_

Making Headlines

Newspapers use catchy headlines to grab our attention. These headlines are followed by topic sentences that lead us into the story.

Example: **Headline – Unemployed Man Now Millionaire**

Topic Sentence – The sole winner of Wednesday's 649 million dollar lottery was a laid-off, assembly-line worker from Barrie, Ontario.

For each headline below, write a topic sentence that might be used to introduce the first paragraph of the newspaper article.

1. Headline: Firemen Rescue Baby

    Topic Sentence: _From Fire_

2. Headline: School Closing Inevitable

    Topic Sentence: _to much money_

3. Headline: Leafs Squeak out a Win

    Topic Sentence: _in an over time goal_

4. Headline: Worst Storm of the Year

    Topic Sentence: _houses ruined_

5. Headline: 9-year-old Boy Praised for Bravery

    Topic Sentence: _Saved his own mother_

CHALLENGE

Here are two topic sentences for newspaper articles. Write the headlines.

1. Headline: _victory fades for paul dewitt!_

    Topic Sentence: With only one lap to go and victory certain, race car driver Paul DeWitt could not have known the tragedy he faced on that final turn.

2. Headline: _Champ under age!_

    Topic Sentence: It took eleven hours and sixteen minutes but with two brilliant moves, Derek Jackson became the first world chess champ on under the age of sixteen.

13 Tips for Effective Writing

Frequently Confused Words

Using a dictionary to clarify the meanings of words is a useful way of ensuring that you are using the proper word in the context of a sentence. Context refers to the meaning of the sentence.

Is this a stationary or stationery item?

Exercise A

In each sentence, choose the correct word to suit the context of the sentence.

1. ___its___ (It's, Its) been a long time since the last time they met.

2. Don't ___accept___ (accept, except) anything from a stranger.

3. ___Whose___ (Who's, Whose) jacket is that?

4. He didn't think the results were ___fair___ (fare, fair).

5. I don't think ___theres___ (theirs, there's) is as cheap as ours.

6. He did not have bus ___fair___ (fair, fare).

7. The school ___principal___ (principle, principal) spoke to the students.

8. The horse came ___fourth___ (forth, fourth) in the last race.

9. He ___passed___ (past, passed) the puck to his winger.

10. The builder chose the best ___site___ (sight, site) for the location of the new house.

11. She wrote in her ___diary___ (dairy, diary) every day.

12. He bought a ___stationery___ (stationary, stationery) bicycle for exercising at home.

13. The scarf was ___loose___ (loose, lose) around the neck.

14. They walked ___through___ (thorough, through) the dark tunnel.

15. The ___patience___ (patients, patience) waited in the doctor's office.

16. After he hit his head, he was not ___conscious___ (conscience, conscious).

17. She received many birthday ___presents___ (presence, presents).

18. She was asked to ___cite___ (cite, sight) a verse from the poem.

19. The ___waste___ (waist, waste) was put into a garbage bin.

20. He was taller ___than___ (then, than) his twin brother.

Padded Language is the use of unnecessary words or phrases in a sentence. Often these words are redundant (a repeat of a word or idea in a sentence) and should always be avoided. In some cases, a phrase can be replaced by a single word giving clearer meaning.

Example (1): Myself, I like riding my bicycle.
The word "myself" is unnecessary and redundant since the subject is the pronoun "I".

Example (2): In my opinion, I think that it is a good idea.
The phrase "in my opinion" is redundant because it is already stated in the sentence that "I think" is an opinion.

Exercise B

Spot the incidence of padded language and correct the sentences.

Some words that would replace wordy phrases in some of the sentences below are: "if", "before", "because", and "what".

1. In spite of the fact that he called to say he would be late, we were disappointed.
   _____ *are* _____

2. Prior to his time here at this school, he attended another school in the neighbourhood.
   _____ *this* _____

3. I am of the opinion that we should share the expenses.
   _____ *found* _____

4. The novel that is called Lord of the Flies is about some boys stranded on a tropical island.
   _____ *is* _____ *are* _____

5. That car is the kind of car my dad himself wants to buy.
   _____ *wants* _____

6. Recent up-to-date music is what he listens to.
   _____ *modern* _____

7. In the event that he phones while I'm out, please take a message.
   _____ *calls* _____

8. This store did not sell the sort of thing I myself was in fact looking for.
   _____ *myself* _____

9. Due to the fact that the trip was cancelled, the children were disappointed.
   _____ *can colation* _____

Faulty Sentence Construction

Dangling Modifiers

When constructing a sentence, we need to keep modifiers close to the words they modify to avoid confusion.

Example: I saw the school bus walking down the street.

In this sentence there is the implication that the school bus was walking down the street.

While I was walking down the street, I saw the school bus.

This sentence is much clearer in meaning because the word "I" was placed close to the participle "walking".

Exercise C

Rewrite the following sentences with dangling and misplaced modifiers.

You may add words and change the order of words in a sentence.

1. While riding my bicycle, the music on my Walkman entertained me.

   I listened to music on my Walkman and enjoyed it

2. She almost spent two hundred dollars.

   Nearly

3. He only referred to three sources for his Geography report.

   _____

4. He recited a poem about travelling the world with his classmate.

   around the world with a classmate

5. Running down the road, my eyes fell on an unusual sight.

   While

Faulty Parallels

A faulty parallel occurs when co-ordinate elements in a sentence do not have a consistent grammatical construction.

Examples: His father is tall, athletic, and a lawyer.

This sentence should read: His father is a tall, athletic lawyer.

Paul enjoys skiing, snowboarding, and to swim in the lake.

This sentence should read: Paul enjoys **skiing, snowboarding**, and **swimming** in the lake.

Exercise D

Correct the faulty parallel in each sentence below.

1. Eating junk food, too much candy, and eating between meals can lead to weight gain.

    eating too much junk food between meals can
    lead to weight gain

2. The teacher not only assigned History homework but also Geography.

    _____

3. It is important to study hard and doing well in school.

    _____ do _____

4. To sleep and eating are necessary for good health.

    _____ eat _____

5. She had learned to write stories and be a poet.

    _____ to _____

> **Mixed Construction**
> Try to maintain balanced, consistent sentence construction.
> *Example*: A place I like to go is where there is a beach.

> This sentence should read: I like to go to a place where there is a beach.

Exercise E

Correct the mixed construction in the following sentences.

1. A stereotype is when someone is put into a group unjustly.

    _____

2. A character trait that I admire is a person who is generous.

    _____

3. The reason I like playing basketball is because it doesn't require a lot of equipment.

    _____

4. The rules of the school expect good behaviour.

    _____

5. Our transportation system makes easier movement from place to place.

    _____

14 The Descriptive Paragraph

Descriptive Language

Many plain words can be replaced with more descriptive words that create vivid images and enhance the reader's visual experience. Descriptive language (adjectives and adverbs) is used to create images (word pictures).

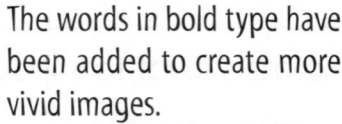
The words in bold type have been added to create more vivid images.

Example (1): The boy walked down the street.
The **cheerful** boy **scampered swiftly** down the **long, narrow** street.

Example (2): The church sat on the corner of the street surrounded by trees.
The **ancient** church **was perched majestically** on the **street** corner **surrounded** by **stately, elm** trees.

Exercise A

Add descriptive words in the spaces below to enhance the sentences.

1. The ___angry___ dog barked ___loudly___ at the ___frightent___ children.

2. In the ___browns___ family room, we sat ___and___ watching a show about ___visnous___ animals.

3. She painted a ___colourful___ picture of the ___mcdonald___ farmhouse in the ___great___ meadow.

4. The ___bad___ odour of ___burned___ cooking filled the house.

5. The ___black___ cat ___had___ chased the ___frigtend___ mouse.

Exercise B

In each sentence below, create descriptive images by changing words or adding details. Replace the words in bold with more descriptive words and add adjectives or adverbs for italicized words.

1. Children **were** in the *park* by the *pond*.

    ___are___

2. The boat **goes past** the *dock*.

    ___went past___

3. The *sun* **shone over** the *mountain*.

_____

4. He **got** *a present* for his *birthday*.

_____

5. In the *forest*, the *animals* **look for** food and a *place* **to live**.

_____

Spatial Order refers to a writing technique where the writer describes details in the order that they appear. Imagine that you are a camera moving around a space focusing on details in the space in the order that the camera picks up the images.

Exercise C

You are in your classroom. Describe the details in the classroom in a paragraph.

Step One: List objects or details that you intend to write about in your description.

Assume that you are the camera and move around the classroom from left to right picking up details. Your topic sentence should tell the reader where you are. Try to include details of colour, size, shape, texture, and position of objects in the room. Use specific descriptions that stimulate the senses (sight, sound, smell, touch, taste) of the reader.

1. _____
2. _____
3. _____
4. _____
5. _____
6. _____
7. _____
8. _____

Step Two: Compose a descriptive paragraph using the objects and details listed above.

Title: _____

_____

_____

_____

_____

_____

From General to Specific

To present descriptive details in the order of general to specific, begin with a topic sentence that tells the reader what you are writing about. Follow the topic sentence with a list of specific descriptions.

Example:

General Topic – Going to a hockey playoff game

Specific Details – shiny, white ice surface; smell of popcorn; people crowding into their seats; music over the loudspeakers; players entering the arena; national anthem

Exercise D

From the general topic sentences below, develop a list of specific details that could be used in a descriptive paragraph. Consider using details that appeal to the senses.

A. Last Sunday, my friends and I went on a long bicycle trip.

Specific details: 1. _____   2. _____

3. _____   4. _____

5. _____   6. _____

B. When I entered the room, the lights went on and everyone yelled, "Surprise."

Specific details: 1. _____   2. _____

3. _____   4. _____

5. _____   6. _____

C. Suddenly, dark, threatening clouds filled the sky.

Specific details: 1. _____   2. _____

3. _____   4. _____

5. _____   6. _____

D. The old house looked haunted but we went inside anyway.

Specific details: 1. _____   2. _____

3. _____   4. _____

5. _____   6. _____

Exercise E

Compose two descriptive paragraphs choosing one of the topics from Exercise D or from the suggestions below.

If you choose from the selections in Exercise D, there is a topic sentence for you to use as the beginning of your descriptive composition. If you choose from the selection below, you will have to write a topic sentence.

Shopping Spree	The Dinner Buffet	Noises in the Night
Our New House	An Unforgettable Adventure	Danger in the Wild

Composition 1

Title: _____

Topic Sentence:_____

_____

_____

_____

_____

_____

Composition 2

Title: _____

Topic Sentence:_____

_____

_____

_____

_____

_____

15 The Narrative and Explanatory Composition

The Narrative Composition

The purpose of narrative writing is to tell a story – true or imagined. A narrative story may be told in either the **first person** or the **third person**. When the story is told from the first-person's point of view, the storyteller uses the pronoun "I" or "we". When a story is told from the third-person's point of view, the storyteller uses the pronoun "he", "she", or "it".

The Process

Step One: think of a general story line
Step Two: narrow your story line down to a more specific topic
Step Three: create a list of events in your story in the order in which they happen
Step Four: write your composition

Exercise A

Choose a topic from the list. After you choose a general topic, narrow it down to a specific topic. Then, write an outline for an introduction that will let the reader know the background of your story (i.e. time and place).

Suggested General Topics:

1. **Holiday Adventure**

2. **A Great Day in Sports**

3. **Alone on Stage**

A. General Topic: _____

B. Narrowed Topic: _____

C. Introduction:

_____

_____

_____

D. Events as they happened:

1. _____   2. _____   3. _____

4. _____   5. _____   6. _____

E. Conclusion: _____

_____

Based on the outline, write a finished copy of your narrative.

Include the following:

1. an introductory paragraph (one or two sentences) that sets up your story
2. two or three body paragraphs that contain the details of the events of your story
3. a concluding paragraph that provides an ending to your story

Title: _____

The Introduction – _____

_____

_____

_____

The Body – (Paragraph 1) _____

_____

_____

_____

The Body – (Paragraph 2) _____

_____

_____

_____

The Body – (Paragraph 3) _____

_____

_____

_____

Conclusion – _____

_____

_____

_____

The Explanatory Composition

The purpose of an explanatory composition is to explain in detail how to do something or how something works. It provides information for the reader.

The Process

1. Choose a topic for explanation: it is easier to write about a process familiar to you; or, to write on a topic that is easy to research.

2. Make a list of points to explain in the logical order they should be revealed.

3. Create an introduction to your composition that states the subject of your composition and makes the reader interested to read your explanation.

4. Write a concluding paragraph that sums up your explanatory composition or asks the reader to think further about the topic of your composition.

Exercise C

Choose a topic. Fill in the information to create a working outline for your explanatory composition.

Suggested General Topics:

1. **Preparing for a Test**

2. **Downloading a Computer File**

3. **Training a Dog to Do Tricks**

Title: _____

Introductory Idea: _____

_____

_____

Points of Explanation:

1. _____ 2. _____

3. _____ 4. _____

5. _____ 6. _____

Concluding Thought: _____

_____

_____

Exercise D

Based on the outline, write a finished copy of your explanatory composition.

Include the following:

1. an introductory paragraph (one or two sentences) that sets up your composition – you may want to mention what it is you are explaining, how important it is to know this information, or how useful this information is in certain circumstances
2. one or two body paragraphs that contain the step-by-step details of the explanation
3. a concluding paragraph that provokes further thought or that is a summation of your explanation

Title: _____

Introduction:

_____

_____

_____

The Body – (paragraph 1: step-by-step points of explanation for first part of the process)

_____

_____

_____

_____

_____

The Body – (paragraph 2: step-by-step points of explanation for second part of the process)

_____

_____

_____

_____

_____

Conclusion – _____

_____

_____

Comma Use

Exercise A

Check each sentence below for proper comma use. Write "C" for correct and "INC" for incorrect in the space provided. Commas may be omitted or placed incorrectly.

1. The boys, played football in the yard. _____

2. They bought the following items: bread, milk, cans of soup, and coffee. _____

3. Incidentally, I'm glad that everyone could attend this meeting. _____

4. Although he was tired from working all day, he helped his friend move furniture. _____

5. Whenever the students finish all their school work they are allowed to read their novels. _____

6. When the wind blows, the rain pours down, and thunder sounds, we go for cover. _____

7. His uncle the local barber cuts hair for all the family. _____

8. People should always be kind, not cruel. _____

9. Indeed it was all they could do under the circumstances. _____

10. It was a dark, stormy night. _____

11. He said, "I'm happy to be of help." _____

12. Both teams, tried their hardest but only one team was victorious. _____

Exercise B

In each of the following sentences, commas are missing. Insert commas where needed.

1. On September 4 2004 they will be attending high school.

2. He asked "Am I allowed to go out this afternoon?"

3. They were told to bring the following: boots gloves a hat and a warm jacket.

4. The neighbour the one who lives across the street asked me to mow his lawn.

5. His uncle Dr. O'Reilly worked at the local hospital.

6. The policeman a tall thin man made a presentation to the students.

7. They stopped for gas for groceries and for directions.

8. Steven the oldest of them all was chosen to lead his group.

9. The runner who wore a green shirt came second in the final heat.

10. However once they are organized they will present our project.

11. Because she woke up earlier than everyone else she made breakfast.

12. Students should be wide awake not tired.

Colon and Semicolon

Exercise C

Insert a colon where needed in each of the following sentences below.

1. They found the following items gold, silver, jewellery, and diamonds.

2. She has one great talent singing.

3. Their team had one main objective play well.

4. Writing children's books was more than an occupation it was her life.

5. He set his alarm for 710 a.m. to get to school before 800 a.m.

6. The article "Driving Across Country The Ideal Holiday" was featured in CAA Magazine.

7. There was one thing that always worried her getting behind in her homework.

8. Don't forget to bring the necessities food, clothing, and equipment.

9. The purpose of the meeting was clear they wanted to agree to work together.

10. The essay stated "The reason that the economy is healthy is because employment is high."

Exercise D

Insert a semicolon where needed.

1. The boys organized garage sale they collected old things from all the neighbours.
2. The weather forecast was grim nevertheless, they went camping as planned.
3. The girls played in the south yard the boys played in the north yard.
4. Never before had they seen such a sight they were truly amazed.
5. The day to move into the new house arrived everyone was excited.

Exercise E

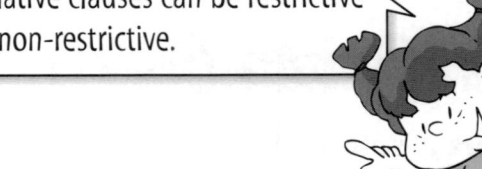
Relative clauses can be restrictive or non-restrictive.

Underline the restrictive relative clauses in the sentences below.

1. The car that was used to deliver the goods broke down.
2. The people who donated food and money were very generous.
3. Before the day began, the people who were organizing the events went to work.
4. The teacher asked the students who had finished their work to help in the gym.
5. They fans cheered for the player who scored the winning goal.
6. The story that was about life on a farm was a favourite of hers.
7. Shoes that no longer fit should not be worn.
8. The animals that live in a zoo are well taken care of.

Exercise F

Underline the non-restrictive clauses in the sentences below and add the necessary commas.

1. The bird whose wings were flecked with red chirped loudly.
2. The students who arrived by school bus were coming to compete in the track meet.
3. Her sister who has the bedroom downstairs is much older than she.
4. The dogs many of which were small played together in the park.
5. The theatre patrons who had parked their cars lined up for tickets.
6. The child who wore a red jacket played on the swing.
7. His friend whom he counted on was a great help to him.
8. The shoppers who were tired stopped for coffee.

Capitalization

Put capitals where necessary in the following sentences.

1. john went to see dr. brooks at mount hope hospital in ottawa.
2. in september, students will return to school until the christmas holidays.
3. they ate in a french restaurant in a small town outside paris.
4. the girl from hong kong spoke very good english.
5. he read a book titled "the bad beginning".
6. he asked, "what time are you expecting me?"
7. professor reid works at the university of calgary.
8. he played in the canadian football league for the b.c. lions.
9. they scheduled the meeting at city hall on thursday.
10. the poem "a vagabond song" was written by bliss carmen.

Quotation Mark

Insert quotation marks in the following sentences. Add or change other punctuation (commas, question marks, capitals) where needed.

One sentence has quotations inside quotations.

1. He asked when will you be coming home.
2. I'm excited said Susan are you.
3. The short story A Day at the Fair was read by the students.
4. She said be on time to which I replied don't worry, I will.
5. The article The Ten Best Vacation Spots appeared in the newspaper.
6. He said I enjoyed reading the story My Best Friend in our reader.
7. The teacher explained look at the hundreds digit first.
8. If you don't do it right he said you'll have to do it again after school.

Frequently Confused Words

Exercise I

Choose the word with the correct meaning for each of the following sentences.

1. He couldn't _____ (here, hear) because of all the noise.

2. This was _____ (there, their) best effort.

3. I don't know _____ (who's, whose) project is the best.

4. He couldn't afford the bus _____ (fare, fair) for the trip.

5. He was asked to come _____ (fourth, forth) and speak to the crowd.

6. He gave a very _____ (thorough, through) account of what happened.

Preposition, Gerund, and Infinitive Phrases

Exercise J

Identify the phrases underlined as preposition, gerund, or infinitive phrases.

> Write "preposition", "gerund", or "infinitive" in the spaces provided.

1. <u>Sleeping in on the weekend</u> is a pleasure.   _____

2. The girl <u>wearing the blue dress</u> sat in the front row.   _____

3. He wanted <u>to swim in the pool</u> on the hot day.   _____

4. <u>Running down the street</u>, he tripped and fell.   _____

5. The boy <u>combing his hair</u> looked in the mirror.   _____

6. <u>Gliding over the water</u>, the boat sailed away.   _____

7. <u>To want something</u> doesn't mean you need it.   _____

8. <u>Across the field</u>, the birds flew in formation.   _____

Padded Language

Exercise K

The following sentences have padded language that needs to be removed. Rewrite the following sentences correcting the wordiness.

1. In my opinion I think that it is important to keep fit.

   _____

2. That game is the kind of game that one would play when one wants to have fun.

_____

3. In the event that the weather is bad we will postpone the event.

_____

4. In spite of the fact that she waited they did not in fact show up on time.

_____

5. Due to the fact that the homework is due tomorrow we must hurry to finish it.

_____

6. You should never repeat the same mistake again.

_____

Faulty Sentence Structure

Exercise L

Identify the faulty parallels and the misplaced modifiers and correct the sentences below.

1. I saw a large dog walking to school.

_____

2. The music played loudly while sitting in the car.

_____

3. He nearly walked the whole way home.

_____

4. She sang a song about friendship with her fellow students.

_____

5. Swimming, skiing, and to go on a hike are good ways to exercise.

_____

6. It is necessary to think positive and being happy.

_____

1 The Sentence and Its Parts

A. 1. <u>The fluffy, white clouds</u> (drifted lazily overhead).
   2. <u>The boy's bicycle</u> (was locked in the backyard).
   3. <u>Boys and girls alike</u> (enjoyed watching the movie).
   4. <u>Cows, sheep, and chickens</u> (shared the same barn on the farm).
   5. <u>To win</u> (is exciting but) <u>to play fair</u> (is most important).
   6. <u>The morning of our first day on holiday</u> (was bleak).
   7. <u>Playing baseball, basketball, and football</u> (are his favourite activities).

B. 1. Complete   2. Incomplete   3. Complete
   4. Complete   5. Incomplete   6. Incomplete
   7. Incomplete

C. (Individual writing)

D. 1. <u>boy</u> ; (ran)   2. <u>current</u> ; (swept)
   3. <u>they</u> ; (changed)   4. <u>car</u> ; (was washed)
   5. <u>they</u> ; (had)   6. <u>wind</u> ; (blew)
   7. <u>Leo</u> ; (saw)   8. <u>I</u> ; (have seen)
   9. <u>boy</u> ; (walked)   10. <u>guests</u> ; (helped)

E. 1. (him) ; <u>puck</u>   2. (us) ; <u>questions</u>
   3. <u>us</u>   4. (us) ; <u>song</u>
   5. (customers) ; <u>gift</u>   6. (Paul) ; <u>question</u>

F. 1. an   2. the   3. an   4. a
   5. an   6. a   7. a ; an 8. an

G. 1. We watched a basketball game in the gym after school yesterday.
   2. Our school team played against the team with the best record.
   3. Although our team fell behind, they did not give up.
   4. They trailed by only three points in the last minute of the last quarter.
   5. Unfortunately, Ken missed the long shot and our team lost the game.
   6. Our team played very well in spite of the loss.

2 Nouns and Pronouns

A. (Individual answers)

B. 1. fireplace   2. father-in-law   3. manhole
   4. dining room   5. swimming pool   6. eggplant
   7. headquarters   8. hairdryer

C. 1. chiefs   2. taxes   3. proofs
   4. armies   5. shelves   6. skies
   7. churches   8. radios   9. keys
   10. heroes   11. patios   12. sixes

Challenge
   (Suggested answers)
   1. Their plural form is the same as their singular form.
   2. cloths – materials made by weaving cotton, wool, silk, etc.
      clothes – things that people wear to cover their bodies
   3. is ; is

D. 1. our   2. we   3. they   4. he
   5. His   6. him   7. he   8. He
   9. it   10. It   11. His   12. they
   13. him   14. he   15. it   16. he

E. 1. that   2. whom   3. who
   4. that   5. whomever   6. that
   7. who   8. which   9. whom
   10. What   11. Who   12. whom

3 Adjectives and Adverbs

A. (Individual answers)

B. 1. chilly   2. sour   3. content
   4. younger   5. positive   6. ill
   7. good   8. happy

C. 1. my   2. their   3. her
   4. our   5. his   6. its

D. 1. fast   2. gracefully
   3. swiftly ; carefully   4. brightly ; quickly
   5. eventually   6. hard ; poorly

Challenge
   (Suggested answer)
   Each of them can be both an adjective and an adverb in a sentence.

E. (Individual writing)

F. (Individual writing)

G. 1. bad – worse – worst
   2. well – better – best
   3. lazily – more lazily – most lazily
   4. useful – more useful – most useful
   5. friendly – friendlier – friendliest
   6. far – farther / further – farthest / furthest
   7. good – better – best
   8. little – less – least
   9. much – more – most

4 Clauses

A. 1. IND   2. IND   3. DEP
   4. IND   5. DEP   6. DEP

B. (Individual writing)

C. 1. The teacher was not happy because our homework was sloppy.
   2. As we approached the beach, we could feel the ocean breeze.
   3. Even if we got up early, we would have been too late.
   4. Because of the snowfall, the cars were sliding off the road.
   5. After we finished eating dinner, we had a delicious dessert.
   6. Wherever we move to, we will buy a new house.
   7. She put on her raincoat even though it wasn't raining yet.
   8. The best team will win the game provided that they play their best.
   9. The school built a new gymnasium because the original one was too small.
   10. It wasn't the best day for a picnic since we forgot the sandwiches.

D. 1. adjective   2. adverb   3. adverb
   4. adverb   5. adjective   6. adverb
   7. adjective   8. adverb

Challenge
   (Individual writing)

E. 1. wherever nature could be enjoyed ; D
   2. where they could park the car ; C
   3. How we could settle the matter ; A
   4. That he could come up with the best idea ; A
   5. whomever they had on their team ; D
   6. when they would be dismissed ; B

Challenge
(Individual writing)

5 Verb Tenses

A. (Individual writing)
B. 1. has read   2. had tidied
   3. will have made   4. has seen
   5. had scored   6. will have cleared
C. 1. past perfect   2. simple past
   3. present perfect progressive
   4. simple present
   5. future perfect progressive
   6. simple future ; simple present
   7. present progressive
   8. future perfect ; simple past
D. 1. caught (TR)   2. thought (INT)
   3. built (TR)   4. blew (INT)
   5. competed (INT) ; didn't win (INT)
   6. rented (TR)   7. sounded (INT) ; left (TR)
   8. go (INT)   9. cried (INT) ; heard (TR)
   10. shot (TR)
E. (Individual writing)
F. 1. rose   2. laying   3. lying   4. set
   5. sitting   6. raised   7. rising   8. raise
   9. laid   10. lay

6 Verbals and Verbal Phrases

A. 1. dreaming (ADJ) ; startled (ADV)
   2. hidden (ADJ)
   3. defeated (ADJ) ; playing (ADJ)
   4. barbecued (ADJ)
   5. torn (ADJ)
   6. opening (ADJ)
   7. swinging (ADJ)
B. (Individual writing)
C. (Individual writing)
D. (Individual writing)
Challenge
(Individual writing)
E. 1. noun   2. adverb   3. adverb
   4. noun   5. noun   6. noun
F. (Individual writing)

7 Direct and Indirect (Reported) Speech

A. 1. He said that he enjoyed a walk in the park.
   2. She said that she was preparing for the test.
   3. Simon explained that he had missed the school bus.
   4. Brian said that Peter had just gone out.
   5. They explained that they had been busy writing the report.
   6. Fiona said that there are now three territories in Canada.
   7. The teacher said that she would be away most of the week.
   8. Marilyn said that she had done all her work.
   9. The girls said that they had been waiting for Helen.
   10. Nicole says that she is never good at swimming.

B. 1. Mr. Smith said that he was starting a new course that week.
   2. Lilian said that she had gone to the dentist two days before.
   3. He told us that the players had stayed in the hotel the previous week.
   4. He said that there would be two new boys joining us the following week.
   5. The teacher said that John had been absent that day.
   6. Ben said that he had seen John the day before in the movie theatre.
   7. The police officer said that the accident had happened a week before.
   8. Julie said that her cousin would come two days later.
C. 1. The children asked how they got there.
   2. She asked me if I had been to Cambridge before.
   3. Shannon asked if I had got a CD player.
   4. The teacher asked Shawn if he had drawn the picture.
   5. The manager asked the applicant if he could use the programme.
   6. The girls asked when they could go in.
Challenge
   Brad had run into Gord the week before. When Gord saw Brad, Gord told him that they were having a practice session after school. He asked Brad if he wanted to join them. Brad replied that he would not be joining them because he had not completed his science project.
D. 1. The captain said to them, "The game will be postponed to next Friday."
   2. I asked, "Do we have to pay for the trip?"
   3. She remarked, "The test is too difficult for the average students."
   4. She said to him, "I like your new suit."
   5. The driver said, "I have been waiting here for more than an hour."
   6. She asked me, "What time will you be home?"
E. 1. The teacher asked the new boy what his name was.
   2. I explained that plants need water, light and earth to grow.
   3. She said she had met John the month before.
   4. Simon said that he had never been to Disneyland.
   5. The teacher asked us if anyone of us wanted to stay behind.
   6. The police officer asked me if I had seen a tall man with a brown briefcase.

Progress Test 1

A. 1. INC   2. INC   3. C   4. C
   5. C   6. INC   7. C   8. C
   9. C
B. (Individual writing)
C. 1. sandwiches (direct)
   2. him (indirect) ; gift (direct)
   3. her (indirect) ; books (direct)
   4. her (indirect) ; question (direct)
   5. answer (direct)
   6. us (indirect) ; story (direct)
D. 1. grandfather   2. textbook   3. high school
   4. floppy disk   5. living room   6. fireworks
   7. mother-in-law   8. water-slide

E. 1. Proper   2. Common   3. Proper
   4. Abstract   5. Abstract   6. Proper
   7. Common   8. Abstract   9. Concrete
   10. Common
F. 1. proofs   2. patios   3. tomatoes
   4. elves   5. chiefs   6. canoes
   7. heroes   8. men   9. moose
   10. pants   11. scissors   12. skies
G. 1. I – me – my ; mine
   2. We – us – our ; ours
   3. They – them – their ; theirs
   4. He – him – his
   5. She – her – her ; hers
   6. It – it – its
H. 1. who   2. that   3. which
   4. whom   5. where
I. 1. (In the heat) of the day, they went (for a swim).
   2. The boys of the sixth grade played (in the yard).
   3. (During the night), the dog in the yard barked endlessly.
J. 1. good – better – best
   2. much – more – most
   3. well – better – best
   4. far – farther / further – farthest / furthest
   5. bold – bolder – boldest
   6. bad – worse – worst
K. 1. Because he won the race
   2. although she left late
   3. Whenever we get together
   4. when the teacher was writing on the chalkboard
   5. Unless you come on time
L. 1. have been playing   2. seems
   3. will continue   4. enjoy
   5. is   6. promised
   7. has made   8. will have
M. 1. transitive   2. transitive   3. intransitive
   4. transitive   5. intransitive
N. 1. Running ; hidden   2. bitten ; swelling
   3. Feeling   4. chosen ; debating
   5. eating   6. To help ; to hinder
O. 1. Kitty asked Paul if he thought she could make the team.
   2. The bus driver said that they would be leaving at two.
   3. The little boy asked where he should go for help.
   4. Betsy asked if she was the one who had sung in their concert the year before.
   5. I explained that the CPU is the brain of the computer.

8 Building Sentences

A. (Answers will vary.)
   1. The children played soccer in the yard.
   2. He arrived here late because the bus was delayed.
   3. They went on holiday in Florida during the summer.
   4. Lauren's brother, Randall, who is 19 years old, attends university.
   5. Kara is a creative dancer who makes up her own dances.
   6. The dog chased the ball which went into the water.
B. (Answers will vary.)

   1. He was the fastest runner and he won every race.
   2. When the game was over, everyone went home.
   3. When the bell sounded, the race was on.
   4. It rained heavily so we ran for shelter.
   5. Richard had the lead role in the school play; he played the prince.
   6. The school parent committee organized a fundraising campaign because they needed money for sports equipment.
   7. In the morning, they met at the bus stop and took the 8 o'clock bus.
   8. The highway was closed because the potholes needed repair.
   9. My dog, which was my birthday present, is cute.
C. (Answers will vary.)
   1. The windows were opened because the night was very warm.
   2. The dog barked because there was someone at the door.
   3. When nightfall came, the moon shone brightly.
   4. After the rain, a rainbow appeared in the sky. It was a beautiful sight.
   5. When the teacher asked everyone to be quiet, there was silence in the room.
   6. Her 80th birthday party was a special event.
   7. The car came to a screeching halt and it just missed hitting the pedestrian.
   8. Hearing strange noise in the dark house, the children rushed out screaming.
D. (Answer will vary.)
   Toronto is a big city located on Lake Ontario in the province of Ontario. It is the largest city in Canada with a population of nearly 3,000,000. Toronto has many theatres. It is the third largest live theatre centre in the world, with New York City being the largest and London, England being the second largest. Toronto has many professional sports teams including the Toronto Blue Jays, which is a baseball team, the Toronto Raptors, which is a basketball team, and the Toronto Maple Leafs, which is a hockey team. Toronto has a new arena called the Air Canada Centre in which the Raptors and the Leafs play.

9 The Comma, the Colon, and the Semicolon

A. 1. She was born on July 22, 1990.
   2. They planted tomatoes, cucumbers, radishes, and lettuce in their backyard.
   3. Laughing, not crying, is the preferred reaction.
   4. Indeed, the need for hard work is something we all understand.
   5. He bought a shiny, new bicycle which he rode to school.
   6. When they arrived at our house, we gave them a warm welcome.
   7. "We can be successful," she proclaimed, "if we work hard."
   8. You must drive in this direction, not the other way round.
B. 1. The car that we purchased was not brand new. (restrictive)
   2. The people who paid their money were guaranteed good seats. (restrictive)

3. The show, which originated in another city, was scheduled to begin next week. (non-restrictive)
4. The team captain, who was selected by a team vote, represented us very well. (non-restrictive)
5. The day that he remembers best was the day that his sister was born. (restrictive)
6. Mr. Randall was a teacher whom we all admired. (restrictive).

C. ✔ 1 ; 4 ; 7

D. 1. Today we purchased many items for the party: balloons, cakes, and soft drinks.
2. He wanted only one gift: a watch.
3. The children had no recess: the rain was too intense.
4. The rule is stated clearly: "Never touch the ball with your hands."
5. When she moved away, it was a sad day: that was the only home she knew.
6. The bag was filled with treats: chips, cookies, candy bars, and liquorice.
7. He was upset at losing the game: in other words, he was very disappointed.
8. After all her effort in preparing for the race, only one thing mattered: being there.
9. She has been dreaming of visiting a place: Disneyland.

E. 1. The referee blew his whistle; the game came to a halt.
2. Children lined up to go swimming; the pool had not yet opened.
3. Summer holidays are a time for travel; we may go to British Columbia.
4. Worrying will do no good; action is needed.
5. We visited Canada's Wonderland; we spent the entire day going on rides.
6. They learned about pioneers; they were interested in the hardships they faced.
7. The playground was covered in snow; there had been a big storm overnight.

Challenge
1. I	2. C	3. C
4. C	5. C	6. I

10 Dashes, Hyphens, Brackets, and Parentheses

A. 1. The summer cottage – the one situated on an island – was our favourite summer place.
2. When the sun went down, we were left with one thing – darkness.
3. The crashing waves, the howling wind, and the huge rocks all spelled one thing – danger.
4. Computers, digital cameras, palm pilots, and cell phones – these are the new electronic toys.
5. The main idea of the story – the fact that a young girl had to go away to a private school – made it interesting for children to read.

B. 1. The under-six-year-olds can play in the ball room.
2. The other children are divided into players and non-players.
3. They had to recount the money because someone demanded a re-count.
4. She lived in a co-op apartment that had a chicken coop in the back.
5. Over one half of the voters supported the pro-economy candidate.
6. He drove a semi-automatic tractor to do one third of the ploughing.
7. He was only thirty-two when he became vice-president in charge of over two thirds of the company.

C. 1. The message read: "Wayne Gretsky (hockey great) will be in charge of forming the Canadian World Junior Team."
2. He proclaimed, "The World Junior Hockey Tournament (many hockey fans consider the best hockey entertainment) is fast becoming popular worldwide."
3. He announced, "The company president (Mr. Forsythe) will address the Board of Directors."
4. The year of Canada's Confederation(1867) was one hundred years before Expo in Montreal.

D. 1. The students in this school (of which I am one) will organize a fundraising campaign.
2. The purchase of new band uniforms (once the money is given) will make a big difference.
3. The Grey Cup (a Canadian ritual) is played in a different city each year.
4. The plan was to (1) hold a meeting (2) choose a leader, and (3) divide up the duties.
5. Follow the road (8 km) to the corner store and turn left.
6. My idea (the plan to create a special group to raise money for the hospital) requires the involvement from my friends.
7. The new student (his name is Jordan) sits next to me.

E. 1. "There are many types of insects including...which are found mainly in the Rain Forest."
2. "The importance of regular fitness cannot be underestimated since..."
3. "When we take matters into our own hands...these are the main issues."
4. "The difference in learning styles can be profound..."
5. "The flight across...took more than three hours and twenty minutes."

11 Varying Sentence Construction

A. (Answers may vary.)
1. To be first in his class in Science and Mathematics was what he wanted.
2. Wearing her best clothes, she went to the party.
3. To be a professional athlete would be a wonderful career.
4. Walking down to the lakefront, we met our friends.
5. Gathering in the park, the class had an outdoor class.
6. Having fallen off his bicycle, he injured his arm.

B. (Answers may vary.)
1. New to the school, the teacher could not find his classroom.
2. Early in the morning, the dew frosted the windshields of the cars.
3. Assembled in the library, the students heard the speeches.
4. Under the canopy, we found shelter during the rainfall.

5. The sports he liked to play at school were the following: baseball, basketball, hockey, and football.
6. Whenever working in the library, he spoke softly.
7. Being tied at the buzzer, the game was sent into overtime.
8. Before reaching the campsite near the river, we walked for miles through the forest.

Challenge
1. You should always take time to express your creativity if you enjoy writing stories.
2. Time should be taken to express your creativity if you enjoy writing stories.

C. (Individual answers)

Challenge
(Individual answers)

12 Paragraph Construction

A. A. 3 ; 4 ; 1 ; 2   B. 4 ; 1 ; 3 ; 2   C. 3 ; 1 ; 4 ; 2
B. (Individual answers)
C. (Individual answers)
D. (Individual answers)

Challenge
(Individual answers)

13 Tips for Effective Writing

A. 1. It's   2. accept   3. Whose
   4. fair   5. theirs   6. fare
   7. principal   8. fourth   9. passed
   10. site   11. diary   12. stationary
   13. loose   14. through   15. patients
   16. conscious   17. presents   18. cite
   19. waste   20. than

B. (Answers may vary.)
1. Because he said he would be late, we were disappointed.
2. Before this school, he attended another school in the neighbourhood.
3. I think that we should share the expenses.
4. The novel, "Lord of the Flies", is about some boys stranded on a tropical island.
5. That is the car my dad wants to buy.
6. He listens to up-to-date music.
7. If he phones while I'm out, please take a message.
8. This store did not sell the thing I was looking for.
9. Since the trip was cancelled, the children were disappointed.

C. (Answers may vary.)
1. While riding my bicycle, I was entertained by the music on my Walkman.
2. She spent almost two hundred dollars.
3. He referred to only three sources for his Geography report.
4. He recited with his classmate a poem about travelling the world.
5. While I was running down the road, my eyes fell on an unusual sight.

D. (Answers may vary.)
1. Eating too much candy and junk food, and eating

between meals can lead to weight gain.
2. The teacher assigned not only History but also Geography homework.
3. It is important to study hard and do well in school.
4. To sleep and to eat are necessary for good health.
5. She had learned to write stories and poems.

E. (Answers may vary.)
1. Someone being put into a group unjustly is a stereotype.
2. A character trait I admire in a person is generosity.
3. I like playing basketball because it doesn't require a lot of equipment.
4. Good behaviour is expected in the school.
5. Our transportation system makes movement easier.

14 The Descriptive Paragraph

A. (Individual answers)
B. (Individual answers)
C (Individual writing)
D. (Individual answers)
E. (Individual writing)

15 The Narrative and Explanatory Composition

A. (Individual writing)
B. (Individual writing)
C (Individual writing)
D. (Individual writing)

Progress Test 2

A. 1. INC   2. C   3. C   4. C
   5. INC   6. C   7. INC   8. C
   9. INC   10. C   11. C   12. INC

B. 1. On September 4, 2004, they will be attending high school.
2. He asked, "Am I allowed to go out this afternoon?"
3. They were told to bring the following: boots, gloves, a hat, and a warm jacket.
4. The neighbour, the one who lives across the street, asked me to mow his lawn.
5. His uncle, Dr. O'Reilly, worked at the local hospital.
6. The policeman, a tall, thin man, made a presentation to the students.
7. They stopped for gas, for groceries, and for directions.
8. Steven, the oldest of them all, was chosen to lead his group.
9. The runner, who wore a green shirt, came second in the final heat.
10. However, once they are organized, they will present our project.
11. Because she woke up earlier than everyone else, she made breakfast.
12. Student should be wide awake, not tired.

C. 1. They found the following items: gold, silver, jewellery, and diamonds.
2. She has one great talent: singing.

3. Their team had one main objective: play well.
4. Writing children's books was more than an occupation: it was her life.
5. He set his alarm for 7:10 a.m. to get to school before 8:00 a.m.
6. The article "Driving Across Country: The Ideal Holiday" was featured in CAA Magazine.
7. There was one thing that always worried her: getting behind in her homework.
8. Don't forget to bring the necessities: food, clothing, and equipment.
9. The purpose of the meeting was clear: they wanted to agree to work together.
10. The essay stated: "The reason that the economy is healthy is because employment is high."

D. 1. The boys organized garage sale; they collected old things from all the neighbours.
2. The weather forecast was grim; nevertheless, they went camping as planned.
3. The girls played in the south yard; the boys played in the north yard.
4. Never before had they seen such a sight; they were truly amazed.
5. The day to move into the new house arrived; everyone was excited.

E. 1. that was used to deliver the goods
2. who donated food and money
3. who were organizing the events
4. who had finished their work
5. who scored the winning goal
6. that was about life on a farm
7. that no longer fit
8. that live in a zoo

F. 1. The bird, whose wings were flecked with red, chirped loudly.
2. The students, who arrived by school bus, were coming to compete in the track meet.
3. Her sister, who has the bedroom downstairs, is much older than she.
4. The dogs, many of which were small, played together in the park.
5. The theatre patrons, who had parked their cars, lined up for tickets.
6. The child, who wore a red jacket, played on the swing.
7. His friend, whom he counted on, was a great help to him.
8. The shoppers, who were tired, stopped for coffee.

G. 1. John went to see Dr. Brooks at Mount Hope Hospital in Ottawa.
2. In September, students will return to school until the Christmas holidays.
3. They ate in a French restaurant in a small town outside Paris.
4. The girl from Hong Kong spoke very good English.
5. He read a book titled "The Bad Beginning".
6. He asked, "What time are you expecting me?"
7. Professor Reid works at the University of Calgary.
8. He played in the Canadian Football League for the B.C. Lions.
9. They scheduled the meeting at City Hall on Thursday.
10. The poem "A Vagabond Song" was written by Bliss Carmen.

H. 1. He asked, "When will you be coming home?"
2. "I'm excited," said Susan. "Are you?"
3. The short story "A Day at the Fair" was read by the students.
4. She said, "Be on time." To which I replied, "Don't worry, I will."
5. The article "The Ten Best Vacation Spots" appeared in the newspaper.
6. He said, "I enjoyed reading the story "My Best Friend" in our reader."
7. The teacher explained, "Look at the hundreds digit first."
8. "If you don't do it right," he said, "you'll have to do it again after school."

I. 1. hear   2. their   3. whose
4. fare   5. forth   6. thorough

J. 1. gerund   2. gerund   3. infinitive
4. gerund   5. gerund   6. gerund
7. infinitive   8. preposition

K. (Answers will vary.)
1. I think that it is important to keep fit.
2. One would play that game if one wants to have fun.
3. If the weather is bad, we will postpone the event.
4. Although she waited, they did not show up in time.
5. The homework is due tomorrow so we must hurry to finish it.
6. You should never repeat the mistake.

L. 1. While I was walking to school, I saw a large dog.
2. While I was sitting in the car, the music played loudly.
3. He walked nearly the whole way home.
4. She sang a song with her fellow students about friendship.
5. Swimming, skiing, and hiking are good ways to exercise.
6. It is necessary to think positive and be happy.